# ON THE CAUSES OF
# THE GREATNESS AND MAGNIFICENCE
# OF CITIES

THE DA PONTE LIBRARY SERIES

Giovanni Botero

# ON THE CAUSES OF THE GREATNESS AND MAGNIFICENCE OF CITIES

## 1588

*Translation and Introduction by Geoffrey Symcox*

UNIVERSITY OF TORONTO PRESS
Toronto   Buffalo   London

© University of Toronto Press 2012
Toronto Buffalo London
www.utppublishing.com
Printed in Canada
ISBN 978-1-4426-4507-3

Printed on acid-free, 100% post-consumer recycled paper
with vegetable-based inks.
The Lorenzo Da Ponte Italian Library

---

**Library and Archives Canada Cataloguing in Publication**
Botero, Giovanni, 1540–1617
[Delle cause della gandezza delle città. English]
On the causes of the greatness and magnificence of cities, 1588 / Giovanni
Botero ; translation and introduction by Geoffrey Symcox.

(Lorenzo da Ponte Italian library series)
Translated from the Italian.
Includes bibliographical references.
ISBN 978-1-4426-4507-3

1. Cities and towns – Early works to 1800. 2. Cities and towns – Italy – Early
works to 1800. 3. Urban economics – Early works to 1800. 4. Sociology, Urban –
Early works to 1800. I. Symcox. Geoffrey. II. Title III. Title: Delle cause della
grandezza delle città. English. IV. Series: Lorenzo de Ponte Italian library series.

HT111.B6713 2012      307.76      C2012-904106-8

---

Publication of this book has been assisted by
the Istituto Italiano di Cultura, Toronto

This book has been published under the aegis and with financial assistance of:
Fondazione Cassamarca, Treviso; the National Italian-American Foundation;
Ministero degli Affari Esteri, Direzione Generale per la Promozione e la
Cooperazione Culturale; Ministero degli Affari Esteri, Direzione Generale
per i Beni e le Attività Culturali, Direzione Generale per I Beni Librari e gli
Istituti Culturali, Servizio per la Promozione del Libro e della Lettura.

University of Toronto Press acknowledges the financial assistance to its publish-
ing program of the Canada Council for the Arts and the Ontario Arts Council.

 Canada Council    Conseil des Arts     ONTARIO ARTS COUNCIL
for the Arts      du Canada               CONSEIL DES ARTS DE L'ONTARIO

University of Toronto Press acknowledges the financial support for its publish-
ing activities of the Government of Canada through the Canada Book Fund.

*In memoriam*
*Eric Monkkonen*
*Student of cities*

# Contents

# Acknowledgments

My first debt of gratitude is to the editors of this series, my colleagues Luigi Ballerini and Massimo Ciavolella, who generously accepted my proposal to translate this neglected text, and then waited patiently for me to deliver it.

I also happily record the gratitude I owe to many of my colleagues: Peter Stacey, for our discussions on various matters Boterian; Andrea Goldman, for helping me unravel the Chinese place names in Botero's text, with patience and good humour; Michael Morony, for identifying the mysterious "Bugiafar" who supposedly restored Babylon (but actually didn't); Debra Shuger and Paul Sellin, for drawing my attention to Sir Walter Raleigh's use of Botero's text; my former colleague John K. Thornton, for help in tracking down the source of Botero's observation in Book I on the curious customs of the people living along the river Cuanza; and Teofilo Ruíz, for help with translating this passage from the Portuguese.

Geoffrey Symcox

# Introduction

Giovanni Botero (1544–1617) is principally known today for his treatise *The Reason of State (Della ragion di Stato)*, published in 1589. It won immediate acclaim as a fundamental work of Counter-Reformation political theory for its supposed refutation of Machiavelli and its reassertion of Christian morality as the guiding principle of politics. It went through several revisions and numerous editions in its author's lifetime. Its fame has overshadowed the highly original, perceptive treatise printed along with it, entitled *On the Causes of the Greatness and Magnificence of Cities (Delle cause della grandezza e magnificenza delle città)*. Botero had published this short essay independently the year before, and he now reprinted it as a pendant tacked onto the end of *The Reason of State*, placing it in the subordinate position it would occupy in every subsequent edition but one.[1] I believe that this ancillary placement of *On the Causes* as a companion piece to *The Reason of State* has meant that scholars have not paid it the attention it merits, and with this translation I hope to rescue it from the undeserved neglect in which it has languished until recently.

---

1  The first edition of *Della ragion di Stato* (Venice: I Gioliti, 1589) did not include it; the second, published in the same year, included it, as did all later editions except the Paris edition (1599), which included a French translation of *The Reason of State*. There appears to be just one later separate edition of *Delle cause* (Milan: Nella Stamperia del q. Pacifico Pontio, 1596).

Mario De Bernardi and Federico Chabod were the first histo-
rians to recognize the importance of this work as a pioneering
enquiry into the principles of economics and demography, in the
1930s.[2] Two decades later the sociologist Paul Meadows described
it as probably the first attempt to define and explore an entirely
new field of enquiry, the sociology of cities and the process of
urbanization. This judgment was seconded by another sociologist of cities, Gideon Sjoberg, who called Botero "the first truly
comparative urban sociologist."[3] Not long afterwards, Luigi Firpo,
the foremost student of Botero's work in the twentieth century,
hailed *On the Causes of the Greatness and Magnificence of Cities* as "a
small masterpiece" for its penetrating economic and sociological
insights.[4] Recently it has been the subject of a perceptive reading
by Romain Descendre, who emphasizes its originality and places it
within the encompassing global vision that he regards as the hall-
mark of Botero's political thinking.[5]

*On the Causes* is indeed a work of precocious originality, mark-
ing a radical departure from the previous Renaissance literature
on cities. In the first place, Botero does not trace out a blueprint
for an ideal urban community, in the grand utopian tradition extending from More to Campanella and beyond. His intention is
strictly practical; it is to examine how real cities work, and identify
the factors that contribute to their "greatness." Nor does his work
form part of what might be called the architectonic or Vitruvian

2  De Bernardi, *Giovanni Botero economista*. He also published a reprint of *Delle cause*
   (Istituto Giuridico della Regia Università di Torino, 1930); Chabod, *Giovanni Botero*,
   301–51.
3  Meadows, "Giovanni Botero e il processo di urbanesimo," 328–36. See also an English
   version of this article, "Giovanni Botero and the Process of Urbanization," 90–5;
   Sjoberg, *The Preindustrial City, Past and Present*, 3.
4  Firpo, "La fortuna di un piccolo capolavoro"; and Firpo, "Giovanni Botero, l'unico
   gesuita 'da bene,' " 81.
5  Descendre, *L'état du monde. Giovanni Botero entre raison d'État et géopolitique*, ch. 5.

tradition of urban literature, which since Alberti's *De re aedificato-
ria* had been concerned with architecture and planning, or since
the work of Francesco di Giorgio Martini in the late fifteenth century, with the design of defensive systems based on the bastioned
*trace italienne.*[6] In *On the Causes*, by contrast, Botero shifts the focus
of enquiry from the *forma urbis* and the geometry of fortifications
to economics, demography, and the political factors that foster
urban development, causing some cities to prosper while others
do not. He also diverges from the preceding literature by broad-
ening the scope of his enquiry from the familiar Renaissance terrain of biblical history and Graeco-Roman antiquity to draw on
evidence from the non-European world, giving his argument a
global perspective.

Yet until the work of the scholars cited above, the significance of
Botero's text remained unappreciated. *On the Causes* was eclipsed
almost at birth by the more substantial and more celebrated *Reason of State*. But for a time it maintained a tenuous independent
existence in translation form. It appeared in an expanded Latin
version by the German Protestant divine, bibliographer, and jurist
Georg Draud (1573–1635) in 1602.[7] Meanwhile it was translated no
less than twice into English, by Robert Peterson in 1606, and by Sir
Thomas Hawkins in 1635.[8] It seems also to have been the inspira-
tion for another treatise on the development of cities by the Italo-
German jurist and humanist Hyppolit von Colli (1561–1612), first
published in 1600 – only two years, it should be noted, before the

---

6   Among the abundant literature on this subject, see Fara, *Il sistema e la città. Architettura
    fortificata dell'Europa moderna dai trattati alle realizzazioni 1464–1794.*
7   Draud, *Ioannis Boteri ... Tractatus duo.*
8   Peterson, *A Treatise, Concerning the Causes of the Magnificencie and Greatnes of Cities;*
    Hawkins, *The Cause of the Greatnesse of Cities.* Peterson had also translated Giovanni
    Della Casa's *Galateo;* Hawkins (1575–1640?), from a family of Catholic gentry, was a
    poet and translator of Latin, Italian, and French works. A modernized version of his
    translation of Book III of *On the Causes* appears in *Population and Development Review*
    11, no. 2 (June 1985): 335–40.

appearance of Draud's Latin translation of *On the Causes,* which
raises the possibility of some contact or collaboration between the
two authors. Like Draud, Colli expanded and adapted Botero's
text, adding chapters on subjects not covered in the original,
and enriching it with numerous fresh exempla and classical citations.[9] Meanwhile in England, Sir Walter Raleigh was also study-
ing Botero's treatise; his *Observations Concerning the Causes of the
Magnificency and Opulence of Cities* is a précis of Botero's text.[10] But
after this, interest in *On the Causes* seems to have faded; although
*The Reason of State* continued to attract commentaries and polem-
ics for much of the seventeenth century, its companion piece fell
into scholarly oblivion.

So my purpose here is, first, to provide a modern English version of this important text; second, to make the case for its semi-
nal significance; and third, to situate it in the context of Botero's
other works, and the intellectual milieu in which he conceived it.

### Botero's Life and Career[11]

Giovanni Botero was born in 1544 to parents of modest means
in the little town of Bene Vagienna, in south-western Piedmont.

---

9   Von Colli, *Hyppoliti a Collibus incrementa urbium: Sive de caussis magnitudinis urbium:
    Liber unus.* The author came from a Protestant family that had emigrated from Ales-
    sandria to Zurich and then to Germany. He served as a diplomat and chancellor to
    Christian I of Anhalt-Bernburg and was the author of several political treatises. See
    also the later edition by Ludolph Georg Lunden, *Johannis Boteri libri tres de origine ur-
    bium earum excellentia et augendi ratione quibus accesserunt Hippoliti a Collibus incrementa
    urbium sive de causis magnitudinis urbium liber unus.*
10  Raleigh (ed. Birch), *The Works of Sir Walter Raleigh, Kt. Political, Commercial, and Philo-
    sophical; Together with His Letters and Poems ...*, vol. 2: 321–9. For example: Raleigh's
    final section, "The Causes That Concern the Magnificency of a City," closely follows
    Peterson's translation of the conclusion to Book III of *On the Causes.* Raleigh's inter-
    est in *On the Causes* seems to be linked to his colonial projects. Echoing Botero's con-
    ception of a civilizing process in which cities were instrumental (Book I, ch. 2), his
    opening statement alludes to the need to "civilize and reform the savage and barba-
    rous lives and corrupt manners of such People," presumably the American Indians.
11  This account is based on Luigi Firpo's article on Botero in the *Dizionario biografico
    degli Italiani* (hereafter *DBI*), vol. 13 (1971), 352–62.

Destined for the church from an early age, the typical avenue of advancement for a talented boy of his class, in 1559 he entered the Jesuit college at Palermo in Sicily, thanks to the influence of a paternal uncle, a well-respected cleric in that city. The uncle's untimely death caused Botero to move next year to Rome, where he was admitted to the Collegio Romano, the chief Jesuit educational institution, pursuing his vocation to become a member of the Jesuit order. He already excelled as a Latinist – although he apparently did not achieve a similar mastery of classical Greek – and demonstrated a precocious talent as a composer of Latin orations, verses, and epigrams, attracting favourable attention from his superiors. But he also displayed a factious disposition and a penchant for intrigue, which displeased the authorities at the Collegio Romano, who punished him by dispatching him to teach in a small provincial college at Macerata in the province of Le Marche. This would be the first of several similar episodes in which his difficult character antagonized his superiors and led them to impose sanctions on him, followed eventually by a pardon, until after two decades they finally decided that they could no longer tolerate his behaviour, and excluded him from the Society.

After a year or so in provincial exile, Botero was allowed to return to the Collegio Romano, where he completed his studies in philosophy in 1565. He was then assigned to teaching positions in France, first at the Jesuit college at Billom in the Auvergne, and then in 1567 at the college in Paris. The experience of living in France made a profound impression on him. Although he had already travelled widely in Italy, exposure to a very different society and culture stimulated the interest in geography and the comparative study of political systems that would characterize his mature work. It also gave him first-hand experience of the bitter religious tensions that divided Christian Europe. Since 1562 France had been ravaged by intermittent warfare between Catholics and Protestants, and Botero arrived as this conflict was intensifying. But once more his turbulent character got him into trouble; after two years in France he was recalled to Rome in disgrace and threatened with expulsion before he could take his final vows, for as a postulant he was not yet a full member of the Society.

Once again his superiors gave Botero another chance, and dispatched him to teach at the Jesuit college recently established at Milan by its reforming archbishop, Carlo Borromeo.[12] In May 1572 he accompanied Borromeo to Rome, to attend the conclave that elected Pope Gregory XIII. This first association with the man who would become a formative influence on his mature thinking was, however, short-lived. Botero soon left Milan to continue his studies at the University of Padua, one of the foremost institutions of higher learning in Europe, where he completed the course in theology in 1577.[13] During this period he expressed a desire to join the Jesuit missions overseas, another sign of the interest in the non-European world that would come to inform his mature work. *On the Causes* is replete with political and cultural information from Africa, the Americas, and Asia – especially China, which was of particular interest to his fellow Jesuits, who admired the power, wealth, and order of the Ming empire and cherished hopes of winning mass conversions there.[14] Botero's avid interest in the non-European world would culminate in the volumes of his *Universal Relations (Relazioni universali)*, which were descriptions of different regions of the globe drawn from an encyclopaedic reading of travellers' and missionaries' reports, published in the years after 1591.[15]

12  Established in 1571 in the Brera, taken from the Order of the Humiliati, dissolved by Borromeo.
13  He did not receive the degree because of an outbreak of plague; it was formally awarded to him in 1583 at the University of Pavia.
14  On the first Jesuit missions to China, beginning in 1583, see Spence, *The Memory Palace of Matteo Ricci.*
15  The first four parts were published between 1591 and 1596. Other volumes appeared in 1605–7. Part five was written in 1610 but was not published until the later nineteenth century. See Headley, "Geography and Empire in the Late Renaissance: Botero's Assignment, Western Universalism, and the Civilizing Process."

After finishing his studies at Padua, Botero was ordered to a teaching position at Genoa, and a few months later he was sent to Milan, to teach scripture at the Jesuit college. Here he renewed contact with the saintly Archbishop Borromeo, cementing the relationship that would alter the course of his life and profoundly affect his intellectual development. But the relationship began badly: in the spring of 1579 Botero delivered a sermon in Borromeo's presence questioning whether Jesus Christ had held temporal power prior to the Passion. This theological faux pas deeply offended the archbishop; in retribution he caused Botero to be banished to a teaching position in the newly established Jesuit college at Turin. Shortly afterwards this humiliation was compounded by the decision of his Jesuit superiors to deny him admission to the Society after his many years as a postulant. The immediate cause given for his exclusion was his refusal to take part in a mission to convert the Protestant population of the marquisate of Saluzzo, not far from Turin, but the real reason must have been his vexatious history of intrigue and disruptive behaviour.

Botero deeply resented his exclusion from the Society he had aspired for so many years to join. This setback placed his future in doubt, but help soon arrived from an unexpected quarter. In September 1580 he returned to Milan, where he found renewed favour with Archbishop Borromeo, who now entrusted him with pastoral duties as vice-curate of Luino, near Milan, and soon, evidently impressed by Botero's literary and rhetorical talent, admitted him to his inner circle and made him his secretary. Botero held this post until the archbishop's death in November 1584. He also joined the Congregation of the Oblates of Saint Ambrose, a brotherhood of priests and pious laymen founded a few years earlier by Borromeo. These few critical years under Borromeo's tutelage, imbibing the militant spirituality of the Counter-Reformation, are clearly evoked in the eulogy of Borromean Milan as a model of Christian charity, piety, and virtue that Botero later penned in Book II, chapter 4, of *On the Causes*.

During this time he composed his first political treatise, *De regia sapientia (On Kingly Wisdom)*, inspired by Borromeo and dedicated to Duke Charles Emanuel I of Savoy (Botero's sovereign, since he had been born in Piedmont). It was written in 1582 and published in the following year. Its explicit purpose was to refute Machiavelli; it followed the traditional model of the medieval Mirror of Princes literature, but in the new key of Counter-Reformation militancy. Citing a wealth of biblical passages, Botero enjoined princes to follow the precepts of Christian morality, fear God, and respect the rights of the clergy or face certain ruin: a theme he would develop at greater length a few years later in *The Reason of State*. This first essay in political theory was followed by two devotional works, *Del dispregio del mondo (On Contempt for the World)*, and *De praedicatore verbi Dei (On the Preacher of God's Word)*, both articulating the profound piety he had imbibed from his spiritual mentor, and the treatise *De catholicae religionis vestigiis (On the Relics of the Catholic Religion)*, in which he asserted that evidence found by Spanish and Portuguese explorers and missionaries proved that Christianity had been known in the Indies and the Americas long before the arrival of the Europeans.[16]

After Archbishop Borromeo's death, Botero left Milan and briefly entered the service of Duke Charles Emanuel I of Savoy, who sent him on a diplomatic mission to Paris, where he remained until the end of 1585. During his stay in Paris it is likely that he encountered the works of Jean Bodin, which were to exercise a powerful influence on the evolution of his political thinking.[17] On his return to Milan he resumed his close ties to the Borromeo family, now as adviser and secretary to the young Federico Borromeo, a cousin of the deceased archbishop, destined by his family

---

16   The full title is *Discorso de vestigii, et argomenti della fede catholica: Ritrovati nell'India da' Portoghesi, e nel mondo nuovo da Castigliani. (On the Relics of the Catholic Religion Found by the Portuguese in India or the Castilians in the New World)* published in 1585 at Milan. Latin original.

17   Chabod, *Giovanni Botero*, 299, 340–1.

for an exalted ecclesiastical career. In September 1586, Federico left Milan for the papal court at Rome with Botero as his secretary and adviser. Through the following year, Botero helped pilot him through the tortuous negotiations at the Curia that culminated in December 1587 when the youthful Borromeo – he was twenty-three years old – was elevated to the rank of cardinal.[18]

Botero would remain in Rome for the next eight years, as Federico Borromeo's secretary, until early 1595, when the latter was made archbishop of Milan and departed to take up his new appointment. The years he spent in Rome represent the most productive period in Botero's intellectual development and mark a decisive shift from the devotional works of his early years towards political issues. Late-sixteenth-century Rome, the centre of resurgent Catholic philosophy and historical scholarship, a focus of European diplomatic negotiations, and a clearing-house for information from the Catholic missions across the globe, provided the intellectual stimulus for the three works of his maturity, *On the Causes of the Greatness of Cities, The Reason of State,* and the *Universal Relations.* His personal circumstances allowed him to draw full benefit from this vibrant intellectual milieu. In addition to the privileged position he enjoyed in Federico Borromeo's household, and the contacts it afforded, from July 1587 Botero also served as a *consultore,* or assessor, in the newly reorganized Congregation of the Index of Prohibited Books, a post from which he could keep his finger on the pulse of the latest developments in philosophy and theology.[19] In December 1587, soon after his promotion to the rank of cardinal, Federico Borromeo was appointed to the Congregation, and quickly assumed a leading role in its deliberations.

At the moment when Botero began working for the Congregation, he and his fellow assessors were faced with the thorny question of how to deal with Bodin's *Method for the Easy Comprehension of*

---

18   Firpo, "Al servizio di Federico Borromeo."
19   Originally set up in 1571, it was reorganized by Sixtus V in Feb. 1587.

*History,* which had recently appeared in Latin and Italian translations from the original French. The Congregation of the Holy Office (the Papal Inquisition) wished to condemn it outright, on the grounds that it was tainted with Machiavellianism, but the more moderate Congregation of the Index felt that publication could be permitted once it had been "corrected."[20] The debate between the two Congregations would drag on for years. This episode confronted Botero once again with the work of Bodin, at the point when he was starting to compose his three major political works.

*On the Causes of the Greatness and Magnificence of Cities* was the first of Botero's ventures into the realm of political and social theory. It was conceived in Rome at the same time as *The Reason of State,* which appeared in 1589, and the *Universal Relations,* whose first volume was published in 1591. All three of these works should be regarded as outcomes of the same process of intellectual gestation; they are thematically interrelated, and they draw on a common fund of arguments and examples.[21] On 10 June 1588 Botero signed the dedication of *On the Causes* to Cornelia Orsini, Duchess of Gallese. Botero had a special reason for dedicating the work to her: as the young widow of Roberto d'Altemps, Duke of Gallese, she was related by marriage to the Borromeo family, and was moreover the owner of the Palazzo Altemps in which Federico Borromeo and his household were residing.[22] At the same time,

20  Firpo, "Ancora sulla condanna di Bodin"; Baldini, "Primi attacchi romani alla *République* di Bodin sul finire del 1588. I testi di Minuccio Minucci e Filippo Sega"; Baldini, "Jean Bodin e l'Indice dei libri proibiti"; Descendre, *L'état du monde,* 35–8, 58–81.
21  Descendre, "Raison d'État, puissance et économie."
22  Roberto d'Altemps (1566–86) was the illegitimate son of Cardinal Markus Sitticus von Hohenems (1533–95), Bishop of Constance and Cardinal (1561), who Italianized the family name, Hohenems, as Altemps. Markus Sitticus owed his advancement to his mother, Chiara de Medici, the sister of Pope Pius IV, who had married Wolfgang Dietrich von Hohenems, a governor of the Papal State. Markus Sitticus bought the property that became the Palazzo Altemps in Rome in 1568. See Alberto Merola, "Altemps, Marco Sittico," in *DBI,* vol. 2 (1960) 551–7. The family connection derives from the marriage in 1565 of his brother Jacopo Annibale d'Altemps, a general who had served Charles V, to Ortensia Borromeo, the half-sister of Archbishop Carlo Borromeo.

Botero also published a short pamphlet on the population of ancient Rome, entitled *How Many People Rome Might Have Contained
at the Height of Its Greatness*, which he would subsequently reprint
as an appendix in some editions of *On the Causes*.[23]

Less than a year later, on 10 May 1589, Botero signed the dedication to his political treatise, *The Reason of State*, setting out his
purpose: to refute the doctrine of what he called the "reason of
state," derived from Machiavelli and Tacitus by certain contemporary thinkers, whose secular vision of politics he denounced
as "inhuman" and "impious." As he had in *De regia sapientia*, he
sought to counter the separation of politics from morality that he
discerned in Machiavelli – and also in Bodin and the French Poli-
tiques, whom he saw as Machiavelli's intellectual heirs – in order
to demonstrate that the success of a prince's policies and the prosperity of his domains could only be assured by following the dic-
tates of Christian ethics.[24] In this work, however, Botero did more
than try to refute the pernicious doctrines of Machiavelli and his
followers: probably influenced by Bodin's *Method for the Easy Comprehension of History* and *Six Books of the Commonwealth*, he analysed
the economic and fiscal foundations of political power, pursuing
the line of argument that he had outlined in *On the Causes*, and
that he would soon expound at greater length in Parts I and II of
the *Universal Relations*. His attitude to Bodin was deeply ambiva-
lent: while denouncing his supposed impiety, Botero borrowed
fundamental aspects of his method.

As with *On the Causes*, Botero's choice of dedicatee for *The
Reason of State* was motivated by considerations of family and cli-
entage: he inscribed his new work to Wolfgang Theodoric von

---

23  It appeared in *Tre discorsi appartenenti alla grandezza delle città. L'uno di M. Lodovico
    Guicciardini.; L'altro di M. Claudio Tolomei.; Il terzo di M. Giovanni Botero. Raccolti da M.
    Giovanni Martinelli. Roma. Appresso Giovanni Martinelli, M.D.LXXXVIII.* Martinelli also
    published *Delle cause della grandezza* in the same year.
24  Cf his invective in *On the Causes*, Book II, chapter 4, against the "miserable worms"
    who follow the false maxims of "reason of state" rather than God's law: Machiavelli is
    clearly the unnamed target here.

Raitenau (1559–1612), the nephew of the powerful Cardinal Altemps, whom he also named in the dedication. Wolfgang Theodoric had been elected archbishop and prince of Salzburg two
years before, and was currently residing in Rome with his uncle at
the Palazzo Altemps, where Botero himself was living. In the best
courtierly manner, Botero's preface lavished fulsome – though un-
warranted – praise on both dedicatees for their political acumen,
their devotion to their pastoral duties, their many public offices
and titles, and the antiquity of their illustrious lineage. *The Reason
of State* was an instant success and quickly won European fame for
its author; it went through four editions in the next two years and
was reprinted another seven times during Botero's lifetime.[25] Its
originality – as with *On the Causes* – lay in its attempts to analyse the
economic foundations of political power, but for the most part it
remained a compilation of received political wisdom infused with
Counter-Reformation morality. As such it attracted a wide following of readers among the political elite.[26] Botero enriched subsequent editions with new material and exempla, and composed a
series of *aggiunte* or additions to the text, but did not modify its
basic argument.

Meanwhile he had embarked on a new project, very different
in nature, which came to fruition as the *Universal Relations*. This
ambitious work grew out of a request by his patron, Federico
Borromeo – perhaps inspired by Botero's earlier treatise on the
supposed relics of Christianity in the Indies and America – for
information on the present condition of Christianity in the world
and the progress of the Christian overseas missions.[27] Botero's

---

25  For a complete bibliography of these editions, see Firpo, "Postfazione" to the reprint
    of *Della ragion di Stato e Delle cause della grandezza delle città*, 16–42. For a modern En-
    glish version, see Waley, ed., *Giovanni Botero. The Reason of State*, which includes Pe-
    terson's translation of *On the Causes*.
26  E.g., the dismissive judgment by Friedrich Meinecke, *Machiavellism*, 67: "Compared
    with Machiavelli, he was a very average mind." De Mattei, *Il problema della "Ragion di
    Stato" nell'età della controriforma*, 50–63, delivers a similar verdict.
27  Botero (ed. Firpo), *Della ragion di Stato di Giovanni Botero*, 16.

resulting enquiry, however, went far beyond the terms of that original request. Part I provided an overview of the physical geography of the world, its continents and principal islands. It was dedicated to the Cardinal of Lorraine, a leading member of the Guise family that headed the Catholic party in France, reflecting Botero's keen interest in the religious conflict then entering its climactic phase there. In its later editions it included the *Relation of the Sea (Relazione del mare),* a short but highly original survey of the geography of the world's oceans and an examination of their physical properties.[28] Part II was devoted to political geography, and consisted of a survey of the world's principal states and empires, ranging from the European monarchies, to China and the empires of Asia, to Prester John and the African kingdom of Monomotapa, and concluding with surveys of the Ottoman and Spanish world empires, and the Papacy, which was for Botero the one truly universal dominion. This part opened with an investigation into "the causes of the greatness of states," expanding the enquiry into the roots of political power and domination that Botero had initiated in *On the Causes* and *The Reason of State.* In Part III he examined the adherents of different world religions – Catholics, Jews, Gentiles, and "Schismatics," as he termed them. The fourth and final part, published in 1596, was devoted to the "superstitions" and "idolatry" of the peoples of the New World, the progress of the Christian religion among them, and the difficulties facing the missionaries who were working to convert them.[29]

The *Universal Relations* constitutes a major advance over earlier Renaissance cosmographies like that of Sebastian Münster; it is no longer simply descriptive, and is far less dependent on the classical heritage of Herodotus, Strabo, Pliny, and Ptolemy.[30] It is loosely

---

28    It is in Botero, *Le relationi universali di Giovanni Botero benese,* 241–56.
29    On the composition and structure of the *Relazioni,* see Albónico, "Le 'Relationi Universali' di Giovanni Botero," 167–84; Descendre, *L'état du monde,* 228–58.
30    On sixteenth-century cosmographies, see Cosgrove, *Apollo's Eye,* ch. 5; Brotton, *Trading Territories,* 169–77.

modelled on the standard report, or *Relation,* that Venetian ambassadors were required to submit when they returned from their missions. In composing his own *Relations,* Botero drew on a wide variety of materials: the travel literature now increasingly available in published collections, ambassadors' reports, and the accounts of merchants and missionaries, to which he had ready access from his privileged position in Rome. Parts III and IV follow his declared purpose of describing the present state of the Catholic religion and its triumphant global expansion, framed, however, in a novel manner, as part of a broad comparative schema of the principal world religions. In Parts I and II, by contrast, his emphasis is decidedly secular; here he opens up a new conceptual field, human geography, and explores the economic, demographic, and territorial bases of political power in a comparative study of states and empires.[31] Once again he demonstrates the interest in the non-European world that had characterized *On the Causes* and in the constituent elements of political power that he had analysed in the *Reason of State.* Like *The Reason of State,* the *Universal Relations* was an instant success, because of its comprehensive survey of political geography and the wealth of information it provided – even though this information was presented sometimes in an uncritical and disjointed manner.[32]

Here I should emphasize once again a defining characteristic of both *On the Causes* and the *Universal Relations*: their non-Eurocentric perspective, and the wide range of information about non-European states and cultures that they deploy. This global vision is less evident in *The Reason of State,* however, because it was conceived as a specifically Christian argument addressed to European princes. In *On the Causes* Botero is critical of what he considers

---

31  Descendre, *L'état du monde,* 279.
32  For Alberto Magnaghi, *Le "Relazioni universali" di Giovanni Botero e le origini della statistica e dell'antropogeografia,* Botero's work was a founding text of the social sciences. Chabod, *Giovanni Botero,* 378–430, rejected this view, arguing that Botero used his sources uncritically. On this question, see Descendre, *L'état du monde,* 274–7.

his compatriots' complacent provincialism[33] and adopts a determinedly broader vision, in keeping with his view of the Catholic church as the one truly universal institution and the Jesuits' role as the bearers of its message to all mankind. The examples he cites in both *On the Causes* and the *Universal Relations,* however, suggest that he was better informed about the great Asian empires – China, Mughal India, the Ottomans – than about Africa and the Americas. China occupies a central place in *On the Causes*: its enormous cities provide his most dramatic examples of urban greatness founded on economic and political power.[34] But because he was writing just as Matteo Ricci's mission was reaching China, and before his reports found their way back to Rome, Botero's chief source was still Marco Polo, by then sadly out of date. He is far better informed about Mughal India, evidently thanks to the reports of Portuguese merchants and imperial chroniclers, and the Jesuit missionaries active since their establishment at Goa in 1542.

This use of examples drawn from all over the world, but especially Asia, would become an even more central feature of the *Universal Relations* than of Botero's earlier works. In successive editions and numerous translations the *Universal Relations* became a standard work of reference for the European political elite, both Protestant and Catholic.[35] But it was destined to be his last major literary undertaking; his subsequent works were mostly didactic, suited to the position he came to occupy as an adviser to Duke Charles Emanuel I of Savoy, after severing his ties to Federico Borromeo. In April 1595 Borromeo was made archbishop of Milan. Botero accompanied him there and remained in his service until late in 1598, when he returned to Rome. There he published two new works, the *Discorso intorno allo Stato della chiesa (Discourse on the*

---

33  E.g., Book II, chs 9 and 12.
34  See especially Book II, ch. 12.
35  It was translated into Latin and German (1596), English (1601), Spanish (1603), and Polish (1609).

*Papal State)* and *Dell'ufficio del cardinale (On the Office of Cardinal).*[36]
But he did not remain for long in his old spiritual home. Early
in the following year he was invited by Duke Charles Emanuel
to join his circle of advisers and act as tutor to the young Savo-
yard princes. He departed for the duke's court at Turin, where
he would spend most of the rest of his life, in an atmosphere very
different from the one that had nurtured him in Rome. Turin
was a provincial capital offering far less intellectual and artistic
stimulus than papal Rome; the culture of the court was military,
aristocratic, and ardently Catholic. Small wonder, therefore, that
Botero's literary production now took a new turn.

Once established in his new environment Botero began a series
of conventional historical biographies – *I prencipi (The Princes)*, re-
counting the lives of Alexander the Great, Scipio, and Caesar –
designed to educate and uplift his princely charges. These were
followed by moralizing biographies of fifteen Christian rulers, *I
prencipi cristiani (The Christian Princes)*, and then by another series
devoted to princes of the House of Savoy – all, naturally, dedicated
to his new patron. In 1603 Charles Emanuel decided to send the
young princes to reside at the court of Philip III at Madrid, with
Botero accompanying them as tutor and moral guide, as part of
a dynastic strategy seeking to establish their claim to the Spanish throne through their mother.[37] This project came to nothing:
when a male heir was born to Philip III in 1605, Botero returned
to Turin with his charges.[38] There he resumed his biographical
and courtly compositions with a volume of lives of contemporary
military leaders, *I capitani (The Captains)*, published in 1607, and
additions to the *Universal Relations*, supplemented the following

---

36  On the connection between this work and the *Relazioni*, see Descendre, *L'état du
    monde*, 258–62.
37  Charles Emanuel's consort was the Infanta Catalina, daughter of Philip II. At that
    time Philip III had no male heirs.
38  Only two of the princes came home: the eldest had died of smallpox early that year.

year by a collection of sayings by famous historical persons.[39] He also composed a variety of poems in Italian and Latin, various occasional pieces and devotional works, and a proposal for a crusade against the Ottoman Turks under the command of Duke Charles Emanuel, dedicated to one of his former charges, the young Prince Maurizio of Savoy.[40]

But by now his health was declining, and he was becoming disillusioned with what he considered Charles Emanuel's increasingly rash foreign policy; in 1613 the duke invaded the neighbouring province of Monferrato in pursuit of a dynastic claim, provoking retaliation from the Spanish governor of Milan and a long, destructive conflict. Botero now largely withdrew from official duties and court life. He died on 23 June 1617, leaving a large part of his considerable fortune to the Society of Jesus. And, according to his last wishes, he was buried at Turin in the Jesuit church, the Santissimi Martiri.

### The Text

Botero's analysis of the causes of urban greatness identifies two decisive factors: one economic – manufacturing or trade, facilitated by good communications – the other political – the presence of a ruler, his court, and the machinery of state. Notwithstanding the wealth of examples it cites from Asia, Africa, and the Americas, the real focus of *On the Causes* is the development of the great European cities in Botero's own time and their relationship to the new political reality of princely power, which he would soon examine in *The Reason of State*. Botero's enquiry centres on the European capitals and trading cities of the later sixteenth century, whose "greatness and magnificence" he believed were linked to

---

39  The *Relatione della republica Venetiana* appeared in 1605; the *Relatione di Spagna* and the *Relatione dello Stato della chiesa, di Piamonte* [sic], *della contea di Nizza, dell'Isola Taprobana* were published with *I capitani* in 1607, and the *Detti memorabili di personaggi illustri* in 1608.

40  The *Discorso della lega contro il Turco* was published in 1614, and *Del purgatorio*, his last devotional work, in 1615.

the emerging bureaucratic structures of the absolutist state and
the expanding reach and volume of European colonial trade. He
is not concerned with independent city-republics like those that
had flourished in Italy and the Low Countries during the Middle
Ages, even though he professes admiration for the proudly independent republic of Venice and at one point goes so far as to as-
sert that free cities are more prosperous and renowned than those
ruled by princes.[41] But this seems to be no more than a passing
aside; he was well aware that a new era had dawned and that the
destiny of Europe's cities was now inextricably yoked to the rising
power of the princely state.

In *On the Causes* Botero registers the impact of these new political and economic realities on urban development. He composed
this treatise at a time of rapid urban growth all over western Europe, the climax of a period of economic and demographic expansion that had begun a century earlier as Europe emerged from the
long depression of the later Middle Ages. This period marked the
first phase in the cumulative process of early modern urbanization
masterfully charted by Jan De Vries, in which the economic and
demographic weight of cities was expanding in relation to that
of their rural hinterlands.[42] Botero's treatise bears witness to his
perception of this dynamic urban growth and may be read as an
enquiry into its causes. This dynamism was particularly evident in
Rome; at the time he conceived and wrote *On the Causes* the city
was undergoing a rapid phase of development under the forceful
Sixtus V, evoked in Book II, chapter 12.[43]

---

41  Bk II, 2: "non si può negare ch'una moderata libertà e legittima franchezza non
    giovi grandemente alla popolazione d'un luogo, e per ciò le città libere sono per
    l'ordinario, data la parità delle cose, più celebri e più frequenti che le città soggette
    a prencipi ed a monarchia."
42  De Vries, *European Urbanization, 1500–1800.* His definition of "urbanization" is at
    10–13.
43  Simoncini, *Roma. Le trasformazioni urbane nel Cinquecento,* ch. 9. Guidoni and Marino,
    *Storia dell'urbanistica. Il Cinquecento,* 627–52, explicitly link Botero's treatise to Sixtus
    V's *renovatio* of Rome.

His treatise also reflects the quickening interest among Europe's cultural elite in every aspect of urban life – social, cultural, political, or economic – stimulated in part by the increasing availability of information about cities in other continents. Besides the abundant travel literature available in collections like those of the Venetian publisher Ramusio, here I would cite the six volumes of Braun and Hogenberg's *Civitates orbis terrarum,* published between 1572 and 1617, or point to the popularity of printed perspective plans and mural sequences of city views, like those in the Galleria delle Carte Geografiche in the Vatican, painted around 1580.[44] Papal Rome was a focal point for the collection and dissemination of this type of information, and Botero's analysis of the factors driving contemporary urban development should be read both in this specific context and in the broader perspective of the growing curiosity all over Europe about the form and function of cities.

The work opens in a conventional theoretical key, giving no hint of the economic, demographic, and political arguments to follow. In the dedication to Cornelia Orsini, Botero first defines the city in theological terms as a *speculum Dei,* a human creation that reflects the infinite grandeur and perfection of the world that God has created, a little world set in the vast created world. Then he offers a secular definition: it is only in cities that human life reaches its highest cultural and social expression. Following Aristotle's *Politics,* in the first sentence of Book I he goes on to define a city as a community of human beings, by nature sociable, gathered together "in order to live happily." From this premise he asserts that a city's greatness resides not in its extent and scale, but in the size and strength of its population. His argument here is

---

44  Elliot, *The City in Maps,* 26–9; Nuti, "The Perspective Plan in the Sixteenth Century"; Ballon and Friedman, "Portraying the City in Early Modern Europe"; Schulz, "Maps as Metaphors"; Gambi, "Egnazio Danti e la Galleria delle Carte Geografiche," and Milanesi, "Le ragioni del ciclo delle Carte Geografiche"; Fiorani, "Post-Tridentine 'Geographia Sacra.' The Galleria delle Carte Geografiche in the Vatican Palace"; Kagan, *Urban Images of the Hispanic World, 1493–1793.*

political rather than demographic: it is the citizen body, not walls and buildings, that constitutes a true city, or *civitas,* and that distinguishes it from a mere agglomeration, or *urbs.*[45]

But instead of following up these theoretical premises, Botero immediately shifts his investigation onto the terrain of history and sociology. He first discusses how cities originated and then poses the first of the series of questions that structure his argument: why do people associate in urban communities? He provides the answer in the next chapter, echoing Machiavelli's account in the first chapter of Book I of the *Discourses.* Cities, Botero says, are the result of the process of synoecism, in which the earliest humans slowly evolved beyond their solitary animal-like existence and gathered in villages, until the moment when a charismatic leader such as Theseus convinced them of the advantages of living in a larger community, united their scattered settlements, and founded a city. In the same way, he notes, Alexander the Great and later rulers founded cities, and then observes that this process of urbanization is currently being repeated in Brazil, where the Jesuit fathers and the Portuguese officials are gathering the indigenous people into communities. From this perspective, cities are the essential instruments for government, for religious conversion, and for what he calls "civil conversation": in a word, they are the instruments of a universal civilizing process common to all of humanity but operating from different starting points and at different tempos in different parts of the world.

Botero then lists four factors that impel people to associate in urban communities: force, authority, the desire for pleasure, and – crucially – the advantages to be gained from city life. In the first instance, the threat of war or invasion compels people to seek safety in defensible places, but Botero is quick to point out

---

45 Descendre, *L'état du monde,* 174–8, points out that the distinction *urbs/civitas* derives from Leonardo Bruni, and is developed in Bodin's *Six livres de la république,* I, 6.

that a secure location alone will not make a city prosperous. The site must offer economic benefits besides, as the case of Venice demonstrates: first populated by refugees fleeing Attila's hordes, it grew to greatness because of its advantageous location at the head of the Adriatic Sea. Then, as an example of cities founded by authority, Botero cites the Romans' practice of conquering their neighbours and transferring them to their own city. And as for cities that grow great because of the pleasures they offer, he cites two cases that he knew well from personal experience, Rome and Venice, both renowned for their beauty, and both much visited. But here his argument falters, for he fails to make clear precisely why it is their aesthetic attraction that increases their wealth and population. As he observes, people flock to both cities to admire their monuments and works of art, but he notes that they also come to transact business, so that the appeal of these cities' beauty and antiquity cannot be separated from their political and commercial attraction.

None of the factors enumerated so far will produce great cities, Botero argues, because neither compulsion nor a secure location can ensure lasting prosperity. Something more is required to make a city great and magnificent. This is the indispensable factor that Botero calls "utility" *(utilità)* and which he links with another crucial factor, the "convenience" *(commodità)* of the site, its accessibility by land or water. These two key terms designate the essential conditions that, according to Botero, are necessary to make a city great and magnificent. Possessing a fertile territory is not decisive in itself, for there are many fertile regions that have no great cities in them – here Botero cites his own birthplace, Piedmont, a very fertile province with numerous small towns but no cities of any significance. Nor is a strategic location or an excellent harbour sufficient in itself to guarantee greatness: Messina possesses a fine harbour but is not a city to measure against Naples or Genoa. Likewise, many cities have excellent river communications but nevertheless remain economic and demographic backwaters.

These observations lead Botero to pose his next question: why do people gather in one place rather than another? It is because of what he calls "the power of attraction" *(virtù attrattiva)* that one place possesses rather than another. This is a key term whose several meanings he develops in the next part of his work, Book II, listing the economic and political factors that constitute this "power of attraction" and thus make a city "great" and "magnificent."

First, he describes how Romulus attracted people to Rome by offering them a place of safety and by granting them citizenship and the right to hold offices. In a striking modern parallel he compares ancient Rome to Calvin's Geneva, another example – abhorrent though it is for him – of a city that has grown by welcoming refugees. He then discusses the Roman practice of sending out colonists to found new cities and concludes that it was demographically beneficial. His argument – which he will expound more fully in Book III – links population growth to subsistence and the availability of resources. For lack of subsistence, Botero says, the poor of Rome could not marry and raise families, so the city's population could not increase, but once settled as colonists in their new homes, with land and sustenance, they flourished and multiplied "like transplanted trees." Next, Botero invokes the power of religion to attract population, citing the classic instance of biblical Jerusalem (whose magnitude he greatly exaggerates) and juxtaposing it to modern equivalents: the triumphant Rome of the Counter-Reformation popes and Borromean Milan, for Botero the epitome of a city that owes its greatness to its sanctity. Finally he suggests that a well-ordered university can function as a powerful force attracting population to a city; his example here is the University of Paris, which he had observed at first hand during his two visits to that city.

The argument now shifts to the specific political and economic factors that are the causes of a city's greatness, leading into a discussion of the connection between urban growth, economics, and state power. For Botero, the most important factor of all is industry, the vital "power of attraction" that above all others causes cities to grow. (The chapter on industry only appears in the first edition of *On the Causes;* in subsequent editions Botero shifted it to Book VIII of *The Reason of State,* replacing it by a brief explanatory note. The original analysis of the fundamental source of the wealth and power of cities was thus transposed into a proto-mercantilist analysis of the economic foundations of state power). Botero explains that raw materials like iron, wool, or silk have little value in themselves compared to the finished products that are made from them; human skill and labour create value by transforming crude materials into useful and beautiful objects. A city that is a centre of manufacturing and is endowed with an industrious population will be great and prosperous, as the cities of Flanders or northern Italy amply demonstrate. Rulers must therefore do all they can to foster industrial development in their cities, or their states, as the Ottoman sultans have done by bringing skilled artisans to Constantinople from other parts of their empire, or as "the great Tamerlane" did for his capital at Samarkand. Rulers should ban the export of raw materials, as the kings of France and England have recently done, to stimulate domestic manufacturing and the growth of an industrious population in their own states. Furthermore the prosperity that a city's industries generate can be amplified by the judicious granting of fiscal privileges and by keeping the level of taxation low, as the example of the great Flemish cities demonstrates. The economic policy of a ruler is of critical importance in fostering and maintaining urban greatness.

Next, in a chapter that ranges across the entire globe, Botero examines how trade makes certain cities great, whether by monopolizing or dominating the production of a valuable commodity, as Calicut dominates the trade in pepper by controlling critical maritime routes, and as Lisbon and Seville control their imperial sea lanes, or by reason of their strategic location, like Hormuz and

Malacca or Frankfurt and Antwerp. (Curiously, he fails to note the decline in Antwerp's trade caused by the war in the Low Countries, of which he must have been well aware.)[46] Good communications are essential for commercial prosperity, and to prove his point Botero chooses two examples gleaned from his wide reading in the travel literature: the great trunk-road constructed by the Inca rulers to unite their domains, and the prodigious network of roads and canals built by the emperors of China. He goes on to praise the wise economic policies of the Chinese emperors, the watchful administration of the Chinese magistrates, and the skill and diligence of the Chinese craftsmen, who carefully train their sons and daughters to follow them in their trades. As a result, China's manufactured goods excel in every respect – an example of sound economic policy for European rulers to follow.

Here Botero's enthusiasm for what he believes to be China's exemplarily harmonious society and enlightened government comes through with great clarity. It is a theme that recurs throughout the text and evidently derives from the laudatory account of China by Marco Polo, his main source. Thus, to cite one instance, Botero's eulogy of the city he calls "Suntien" (Book II, chapter 12), is based on Marco Polo's description of Quinsai, the modern Hangzhou.[47] But his reliance on this source, by now almost three centuries old, leads him into a number of errors. He is unaware that the Yüen (Mongol) dynasty founded by Kublai Khan and described by Marco Polo had been overthrown by the Ming in 1368,

---

46  His source was Lodovico Guicciardini, *Descrittione di M. Lodovico Guicciardini Patritio Fiorentino, di tutti i Paesi Bassi, altrimenti detti Germania Inferiore* (1567). He also failed to note the decline of Antwerp in the *Relazioni*, several years later: Chabod, *Giovanni Botero*, 378 ff.

47  Botero garbles Marco Polo's description by claiming that the river he calls "Polisango" flows into the lake near this city, confusing it with the river Marco Polo called the Pulisangan (today the Lougou), which he described as being ten miles from Cambaluc/Beijing, where it was crossed by a magnificent stone bridge, still standing today and known as the "Marco Polo Bridge."

and he seems to believe that Kublai's descendants still rule China from their capital, Cambaluc. Botero identifies it as the capital of the "Cathayan Tartars" and evidently does not realize that this city and the present capital, Beijing (or Panchin as he calls it), are in fact one and the same. His reading of Marco Polo also seems largely responsible for his unduly rosy view of Chinese society and government and his admiration for the enormous size and opulence of China's cities, which he ascribes to the wise maxims that guide Chinese statecraft: the emperors are forbidden to wage wars of conquest outside their realm, and emigration is forbidden,[48] compelling all the inhabitants to devote themselves to productive labour under the watchful eye of the emperor's officials.

This section concludes with an assessment of the political factors – another form of *virtù attrattiva* – that are the cause of a city's greatness, centring on the relationship between states and their capital cities. Political dominion, Botero says (Book II, chapter 10), is "of the highest importance" in making a city great, for the revenue it brings in attracts merchants and artisans. By way of proof he adduces the regional capitals of contemporary Italy and Germany, the great capitals of classical antiquity, and modern Venice. Here he is thinking of city-republics as models of political dominion, but his real concern is with the capitals of the European monarchical states and the great Asian empires. Powerful sovereigns, their courts, and bureaucracies act as magnets drawing in wealth and population to the cities where they reside. The presence of the highest law courts (Book II, chapter 6), staffed by numerous functionaries and frequented by lawyers, draws a constant stream of litigants, which in turn creates a demand for services. The residences of the nobility function in the same way as a force attracting population (Book II, chapter 11). The most powerful

---

48  Botero's argument here seems to run counter to what he had said earlier (Book II, ch. 3) about the demographic benefits Rome derived from exporting part of its population to colonies.

force of all, however, is the residence of the ruler (Book II, chapter 12), which attracts officials and aspirants to office and draws in a perpetual stream of revenue. Botero chooses the evidence in support of this contention from all over the world: from ancient Egypt and the Near East, the Asian empires of the Mughals and the "Cathayan Tartars," China and the Ottomans, Morocco and North Africa. Ethiopia provides a counter-example: there are no great cities in that country because the court of the Negus is a peripatetic tent city, grand in scale but constantly on the move. Botero concludes his argument with two examples very dear to him: Paris, the seat of the kings of France and the capital of Europe's largest kingdom, and Rome, which owes its splendour to the authority and liberality of the popes who rule it.

Finally in Book III and the short treatise on Rome's population that follows it, Botero addresses a fundamental question that he had hinted at earlier: why do the populations of cities – or by extension of the entire globe – not go on growing for ever? Why do they reach a certain level and then stop? Botero's interest in population statistics is not entirely original; Giovanni Villani, the fourteenth-century Florentine chronicler, had tabulated the population of his native city, and Marco Polo had recorded statistics from China, while Bodin devoted a chapter of the *Six Books of the Republic* to the question of demography.[49] Botero's originality resides in his demonstration of the linkage between population and resources, anticipating the argument Malthus would make two centuries later. According to Botero, the population of a city, as also of the whole world, will increase only as long as it has adequate means of subsistence. When the cost of importing provisions becomes too high, and the food supply can expand no further, the city's inhabitants will no longer be able to marry and have children, and the population must stagnate or fall. The same

---

49  Book VI, ch. 1 of Bodin, *Les six livres de la république*, vol. 6: 8–13.

applies to the world as a whole. Conflicts over land and resources, whether between individuals or nations, are therefore the most basic and the most brutal. Poverty and the desperation it breeds are the root causes of crime and war. Botero now poses his final question: how then is the harmony of life in a city to be preserved? In tune with all that has gone before, his answer combines the moral and the practical: through justice, peace, and a ready supply of cheap food.

# Note on the Translation

For this translation I have used the text established by Luigi Firpo, *Della ragion di Stato di Giovanni Botero con tre libri Delle cause della grandezza delle città, due aggiunte e un discorso sulla popolazione di Roma* (Turin: UTET, 1948). Firpo's text is based on the Venetian edition of 1598, the last one revised and corrected personally by the author (see his "Nota critica," 457–69). It includes the dedication to Cornelia Orsini and the short treatise on the population of ancient Rome, but (as in the 1598 edition) does not include the chapter *On Industry* which formed Book II, chapter 7 in the original edition and which Botero later transposed to *Della ragion di Stato,* as Book VIII, chapter 3. For this translation I have restored it to its original place.

I have left the biblical citations in Book II in Latin, as they are in Botero's text. The translations of these passages in the footnotes are taken from the Douai English Bible of 1582.

# ON THE CAUSES OF
# THE GREATNESS AND MAGNIFICENCE
# OF CITIES

# Dedication[1]

*To the Most Illustrious and Excellent Lady,*
*Donna Cornelia Orsini di Altemps, Duchess of Gallese etc.*[2]

Since among the works that His Divine Majesty has created beneath the heavens man is the noblest and worthiest, so then among the outward works of man there is none greater than the city; for man being by nature sociable and desirous to share his goods, it is in cities that conversation and the mutual exchange of all the things that concern life attain their highest form. Here are manufacturing, crafts, and trade; here is the stage on which justice, strength, liberality, magnificence, and the other virtues are practised for the common good, and where they shine forth with the greatest glory. In sum, cities are like little worlds constructed by man within the great world created by God, and just as the contemplation of Nature leads to recognition of the greatness of God, in the same way the study of cities affords a special sign of

1   This dedication does not appear in most subsequent editions published with the *Reason of State*. In the Peterson translation it is replaced by a dedication to Sir Thomas Egerton, Lord Ellesmere. It does not appear in the Hawkins translation.
2   Widow of Roberto Sittico d'Altemps, illegitimate son of Cardinal Markus Sittich von Hohenems (Italianized as Altemps), bishop of Constance. His brother Jacopo Annibale had married Ortensia Borromeo, the half-sister of Carlo Borromeo, archbishop of Milan 1559–84, canonized in 1610.

man's excellence, which in turn redounds to the glory of God, Whose creature he is.

This has moved me, because of the various travels it has been my lot to undertake over these past years, to investigate the reasons why one city is greater than another. And now that I am ready to entrust my treatise to the printer, I am moved to honour it with the very noble name of Your Excellency, as a person for whom it is particularly suited in many ways. It befits your exalted blood and high lineage, because it treats of noble matters; it befits your many titles and estates, because it deals with the foundation and growth of cities; it befits your noble intellect, because it discusses the greatest affairs that can fall to the councils of princes; it befits the solitary state in which Your Excellency now lives, with exemplary constancy and courage at such a youthful, verdant age, because it offers you in a short compendium all that is great and magnificent in the world, so that you need not leave your residence; it befits your piety and religious faith, because it displays as it were a great field that reveals the infinite providence of God, Who like the best of shepherds feeds the innumerable flocks of His rational sheep within the walls of vast cities. Nor does the littleness of this thing deter me, for the smaller and more insignificant it is, the more suited and fit it is to reveal and make manifest Your Excellency's incomparable benevolence.

What is greater than the sun? Yet nowhere are the force of its light and heat better demonstrated than in the concave space of a tiny mirror. But even though my little work may be found wanting in every respect, I am certain that you will welcome it with a serene gaze and particular pleasure, at least because it issues from the household of the Lord Cardinal Borromeo, under the favour of the most illustrious of the Altemps.[3] I beseech the Lord God

---

3    Botero was at this time a member of the household of Cardinal Federico Borromeo (1564–1631), the nephew of Carlo Borromeo.

to grant Your Excellency every happiness, and I very humbly kiss
your hand.

From my house, on the tenth day of June [1588].
Your Excellency's most devoted servant,
*Giovanni Botero.*

# BOOK I

# 1. What Is a Great City

A city is defined as a gathering of people drawn together in order to live happily,[4] and the greatness of a city does not consist in the extent of its site or the circumference of its walls, but in the number of its inhabitants and their strength. Now, men are gathered together through authority, or force, or pleasure, or the utility that results from it.

# 2. On Authority

Cain was the first founder of cities, but the poets (followed in this by Cicero) recount that in ancient times human beings were scattered here and there through the mountains and the plains, and led a life not much different from that of the animals, without laws, common customs, or any kind of civil conversation. Then certain persons appeared, who having acquired authority and a marvellous reputation among their fellows by reason of their wisdom and eloquence, showed the rough multitudes the many great benefits they would enjoy from the mutual exchange of everything if they gathered in a single place and united in a single body. In this way they first founded hamlets and villages, then towns and cities, which caused those same poets to pretend that Orpheus and Amphion[5] tempted the beasts, the forests and the rocks to follow them, meaning by this invention to show how coarse were the minds of those people, and how crude their customs. Setting aside these fables, however, we read that Theseus, after he came to rule over the Athenians, resolved to unite all the people, who

---

4  Peterson amplifies this opening sentence: "A Citty, is sayd to be an assembly of people, a congregation drawn together, to the end they may thereby the better liue at their ease in wealth and plenty."

5  Two mythical poet-musicians; Amphion was the supposed founder of Thebes.

were then living in villages scattered through the countryside, into one city. This he easily accomplished, by showing them the great benefit this would bring.

A similar thing is being done constantly in Brazil, whose people live scattered here and there in caves or in huts built from the branches and fronds of palm trees, and not in houses. Because they live dispersed like this, the people retain their savage mentality and their rude customs, which makes it hard to preach the Gospel, convert unbelievers, instruct those who are gradually converted, and bring them under civil government. So the Portuguese and the Jesuit Fathers use every means to gather them together in the most suitable places, where, following a civilized manner of life, they may be more easily instructed in the Christian faith by the Fathers, and governed by the king's officials.[6]

We can place under this heading too those cities that were built through the power and populated at the command of great princes or famous republics. The Greeks and the Phoenicians founded an infinite number of cities, and Alexander the Great and other kings founded many others, as witness all the cities named Alexandria, Ptolemais, Antioch, Lysimachia, Philippopolis, Demetrias, Caesarea, Augusta, Sebastia, Agrippina and Manfredonia, or in our own day, Cosmopolis, and the City of the Sun.[7] But in this no one is more worthy of praise, after Alexander the Great, who founded over seventy cities, than King Seleucus who, among the many cities he founded, built three named Apamea in honour of his wife, five named Laodicea in memory of his mother, and five named Seleucia in his own honour, making more than thirty in all.[8]

---

6   The editions of 1588, 1589, and 1590 add: "as has been done at Pernambuco, Piratininga, San Salvador, Portosecuro and other places."

7   Cosmopolis was the original name for the city founded by Duke Cosimo I of Tuscany on the island of Elba in 1546, subsequently known as Portoferraio. It is not the utopian community described by Tommaso Campanella in his treatise of 1602, but another ideal city proposed by Grand Duke Francesco of Tuscany, ca 1585.

8   Botero presumably refers to Seleucus I (ca 358–280 BCE), founder of the Seleucid empire. Some of these cities were in fact founded by Seleucus's successors.

## 3. On Force

Through force and necessity people gather together in a place when the threat of some imminent danger, generally war, or massacre, or irreparable devastation, impels them to seek safety for their lives or their property. Such safety is to be found in rugged, mountainous places, or marshes, or islands and other secluded places which are not easily accessible. After the Flood, fearing another catastrophe like it, people sought safety by building their habitations on the peaks of the mountains, or by constructing towers of unbelievable height that reached up to the heavens. And undoubtedly for this reason the cities built on mountains are the noblest for their antiquity, and towers are the oldest form of buildings that have ever been used. But after the fear of another flood had passed, people started to come down and build their dwellings in the plains, until the fear of the arms and the invasion and terror of cruel, savage peoples forced them to flee once more to mountaintops or islands in the sea, or marshes and suchlike places.

When the Moors invaded Spain and reduced it to miserable servitude, those who survived the carnage withdrew to the highest mountains of Biscay and Aragon, while others sailed to take refuge in the Island of the Seven Cities (so called because seven bishops settled there with their followers). The destruction wrought by the great Tamerlane[9] caused the people of Persia and the neighbouring countries to abandon their ancestral lands and flee like stray birds, some to the mountains of the Taurus and the Antitaurus, others to the islands of the Caspian Sea. And just as the invading Slavs forced the inhabitants of Istria to withdraw to the island of Capraria, where they founded the city of Justinopolis,[10] so in the

---

9   Timur, the Turco-Mongol conqueror (1336–1405). Samarkand was the captial of his
     empire.
10  Today Kopar or Capodistria in Slovenia.

same way the Lombard invasion of Italy forced the inhabitants of Transpadane Gaul[11] to seek refuge in the marshlands, where they built the city of Crema.

But because the strength of these places was not usually matched by any great territorial or commercial advantages, or any inducement to settle and remain, there have never been very famous cities there. But if the places into which people are compelled to withdraw out of necessity offer some important benefit besides security, they will easily gain in population, wealth and habitations. In this way many cities in Barbary and the Levant, particularly Thessalonika and Rhodes, have become great because of the large numbers of Jews expelled from Spain by King Ferdinand, and from Portugal by King Manuel. In our own time the flight of rebels against the Catholic King[12] from the Low Countries has increased the population and trade of many cities in England, most of all London, to which thousands of families have fled. About the year of Our Lord 900, while the Saracens were ravaging Genoa and its region with fire and sword, Pisa grew to an unbelievable extent, because the strength of its location was matched by the fertility of its surrounding territory, and access for trade. When Attila invaded Italy, the people of Lombardy, terrified by the horrible devastation he wrought, fled to the little islands of the Adriatic coast, and built various hamlets and communities there. And later when King Pepin[13] made war on them they abandoned the less secure places like Aquileia, Heraclea, Palestina and Malamocco, and withdrew in a body to the area near Rialto;[14] and in this way Venice grew great.

---

11   The Latin name for the central Po valley.
12   Philip II of Spain.
13   Pepin the Short (ca 711–68), the father of Charlemagne, attacked the Lombards in northern Italy in 754.
14   The central district of the present city of Venice.

## 4. On Laying Waste the Lands of Neighbours

To make their own country great by every possible means, the Romans made judicious use of force, totally ruining the lands of their neighbours, so that they would be compelled to leave their homelands and settle in Rome. In this way King Tullus Hostilius destroyed the very powerful city of Alba Longa, King Tarquinius Priscus razed to the ground Corniculum, a very rich place, and King Servius Tullius made Pometia into a desert. And in the time of their freedom,[15] the Romans destroyed Veii, a city of such size and strength that it fell with great difficulty only after a siege of ten years, and even then it was taken by guile rather than assault. Now because these peoples, and others like them, no longer had anywhere to live their lives in safety, they were forced to abandon their homelands for Rome, which thus grew wondrously in wealth and population.

## 5. On Removing Peoples from Their Own Countries to Our City

To increase the size and population of their city the Romans employed a very similar method to the one just described, but rather gentler, which was to transfer all the conquered peoples, or most of them, to Rome. In this way Romulus moved the Cenensi, the Antennati and the Crustumini to the city. But no people brought a greater increase to the city than the Sabines, because after first fighting a long, bitter war they finally made a treaty by which Tatius, their king, was to come to live in Rome with his people. This he did, and the Capitol and the Quirinal Hill were chosen to be

15    After the expulsion of the Etruscan kings, traditionally in 510 BCE.

his residence. Ancus Martius[16] dealt in the same way with the Latins, whom he transferred from their cities of Politorium, Tellena and Ficana, and to whom he assigned the Aventine Hill. The great Tamerlane too expanded the great city of Samarkand by transferring to it the wealthiest people from the cities he conquered, and to enrich Constantinople the Ottoman sultans have transported thousands of families, mostly skilled workers, from the cities they conquered to live there, as Mehmet II did with people from Trebizond, Selim I from Cairo, and Suleiman from Tauris.[17]

## 6. On Pleasure

People also gather together in order to enjoy the pleasures afforded either by a place's site or its artistic beauty. The site, for its cool breezes, pleasant valleys, thick forests, good hunting grounds, and abundant water: Antioch and Damascus in Syria, Bursa in Bythinia, Cordova and Seville in Spain, and other places besides, are endowed with these good things. In the domain of art are the city's straight streets and its fine buildings, magnificent for the skill and the materials with which they are made, and also with magnificent theatres, amphitheatres, porticoes, circuses, hippodromes, fountains, statues, paintings, and similar excellent and wonderful things.

People came to the city of Thespiae for its excellent statue of Eros, Samos for the amazing size of its temple, Alexandria for the Pharos, Memphis for the pyramids, Rhodes for the Colossus, and how many should we believe would have gone to Babylon to see

16   King of Rome ca 640–16 BCE.
17   Sultans Mehmet II (r. 1444–81), Selim I (r. 1512–20), Suleiman I (r. 1520–66). "Tauris" is the classical name of Tabriz, the capital from 1501 to 1545 of the Persian Safavid state, occupied several times in the sixteenth century by the Ottomans.

its wondrous walls? The Romans gladly went to spend time at Syracuse, Mytilene, Smyrna, Rhodes, and Pergamum, drawn by the sweetness of the air and the beauty of those cities. In short, all that feasts the eyes, delights the senses, and entertains curiosity; all that has something novel, unusual, extraordinary, wonderful, grand, or finely wrought, falls under this heading.

Of all the cities in Europe, Rome and Venice are the most frequented because of the pleasure they offer to those who behold them, the former for the stupendous remains of its ancient greatness, the latter for the splendour of its present magnificence. Rome astonishes and delights the mind by the vastness of its aqueducts, baths and colossi; by the masterpieces in bronze and marble, the work of the greatest artists, that can be admired there; by the height and size of its obelisks, the number and variety of its columns, the fineness and diversity of its rare types of marble, brocaded and African, porphyry and alabaster, white, black, milk-white, yellow and variegated, of serpentine and breccia, of its sacred portals, and of so many other kinds that it would be hard to count them and impossible to distinguish between them. What shall I say of the triumphal arches, the Septizonium,[18] the temples, and so many other marvels? And how can we imagine what Rome was like when it flourished and triumphed, if even now when it is brought low, and is little more than its own burial place, it encompasses us and feeds us insatiably with its own ruins?

Venice, on the other hand, inspires no less admiration for its miraculous site, seemingly created by Nature to rule the waters and set limits to the sea; for the size of its incomparable Arsenal and its profusion of vessels, warships, merchantmen and passenger craft; for its endless variety of machinery and devices, munitions and all kinds of naval equipment; for the height of its towers, the richness of its churches, the splendour of its palaces, the beauty of its

---

18  A large ornamental facade screening part of the Palatine Hill in Rome, possibly functioning also as a calendar, dating from 203 CE.

squares, and the variety of its crafts; the good order of its government; and the beauty of its people of either sex, which dazzles the
eyes of all who behold them.

# 7. On Utility[19]

This is so powerful a reason for people to come together in one
place that the other causes would not be sufficient to make any
city great, without the action of this one. Authority is not enough,
because people who are gathered together by the authority of another person will not remain in that place, if it does not offer convenience. Nor is necessity a sufficient cause, because communities
of people grow and multiply over many years, whereas necessity
involves violence, which cannot produce lasting effects. The result is that not only do such cities fail to grow, but also that states
and dominions acquired through mere force and violence do not
last long. They are like torrents that rise and fall in an instant,
without warning, because they have no source, as rivers have, that
provides a steady supply of water; in their sudden spates they may
be dangerous to travellers, but then they dwindle to such a degree
that one may cross them dryshod. Such were the conquests of the
Tartars, who ravaged Asia so many times, or Alexander the Great,
Attila, the great Tamerlane, and the French kings Charles VIII and
Louis XII.

The reason for this is that our nature is so attached to comfort
and convenience that it cannot make do or be satisfied with mere
necessities. Since plants, even if firmly rooted in the soil, cannot
long survive without the benign influence of the heavens and the
benefit of rain, so in the same way communities of men that originate from bare necessity do not subsist for long if they do not

---

19    Peterson translates this as "Of Profite," Hawkins as "Of Utilitie."

benefit from convenience as well. Pleasure and enjoyment count
for much less, because mankind is born to labour; the majority of
men attend to their business, while the idle are few and of no account, and their idleness is sustained by the labour and industry
of those who work. Pleasure cannot subsist without convenience,
whose offspring in a sense it is.

Assuming now that utility is the principal cause that promotes
the greatness of cities, and that utility is not a simple thing, of
a single form, but assumes different forms and manners, it now
remains for us to see what kind of convenience or utility is best
suited to achieve the end we are discussing. Let us say then that to
make a city great, the convenience of the site, the fertility of the
land, and the ease of communication are all of great importance.

## 8. On the Convenience of the Site[20]

I call a site convenient if it is so situated that many peoples need
it for trade, either exporting the goods of which they have a sur-
plus, or importing those that they lack. Since this site is situated
between the former and the latter, it partakes in the trade as an
intermediary and draws profit from these extremes. I said that it
mediates between the extremes, for otherwise there is no reason
for a city to become great, and it will remain empty, or merely
serve as a way-station. Derbent, a city at the Caspian Gates, is situated in a place that is essential for going from Persia into Tartary,
or from Tartary into Persia, yet even so it has never become a great
city, and in our day is of little consequence. This is because it plays
no part in the trade between extremes, but serves only as a point
of transit receiving the people passing to and fro, not merchants

---

20   "Commodità" in the original; Peterson translates it as "Commoditie," Hawkins as
      "Conveniencie."

and men of business, but wayfarers and travellers. In sum, it is located in a site that is necessary, but not useful.

For the same reason, in the valleys of the Alps, which largely surround Italy, even though the French, the Swiss, the Germans and the Italians are constantly passing through, there is no city of middling importance, let alone of consequence. The same can be said of many other sites. Those coming from the Indies through the Red Sea to Cairo must pass through Suez. The islands of São Jorge, La Palma and Terceira are essential to the Portuguese and the Spaniards for sailing to the Indies, Brazil and the New World, yet nonetheless there is not, nor will there ever be an important city in these places. Nor will there be one in the islands between Denmark and Sweden, and between the North Sea and the Baltic. Flushing is no more than a little place, even though it is situated in a position that is vital for the trade between the Flemings and the English and other peoples. Genoa, in contrast, is a great city, and so is Venice, because they both mediate between extremes; they are not just transit-points, but warehouses and stores, as are Lisbon and Antwerp, and others too. It is not enough, therefore, for the site to be necessary, in order to render a city great; besides that, it must be useful to the neighbouring peoples as well.

## 9. On the Fertility of the Land

The second reason for a city's greatness is the fertility of the country around it. Since human life depends on food and clothing, which are obtained from what the land produces, the fertility of its territory is by no means an insignificant factor. And this is all the more so if the land is so fertile that it not only supplies the wants of its inhabitants but also aids the people nearby. Since every land does not produce everything, the richer the territory is and the more it produces, the more it will be sufficient and able to make a city great, because that city will have less need of others, which forces people to leave their homes, and will have more to give to other peoples, which draws the neighbours into our own country.

But the fertility of the land alone is not sufficient to make a city great, because we see there are many very bountiful provinces without a single big city. Such for example is Piedmont, for it surpasses every region of Italy in abundance of grain, meat, wine and all kinds of excellent fruit, with which it sustained the troops and armies of Spain and France for so many years.[21] In England too, although the countryside is very productive, there are no cities worthy of being called great, apart from London. Nor is there in France, except for Paris, which however is not situated in the richest part of this vast realm, for its territory is less pleasant than Touraine; less bountiful than Saintonge and Poitou; less varied in the fruits it produces than Languedoc; less convenient for the sea than Normandy; less abundant in wine than Burgundy and in grain than Champagne, and in both than the territory of Orleans; less abundant in meat than Brittany and the province of Bourges. A fertile territory is not enough, therefore, to make a city great. The reason is this: if a country is rich and productive its inhabitants find everything that is useful and necessary at home, and so do not care to travel elsewhere; they enjoy everything without effort where it grows, since people love their comforts, with as little inconvenience as possible. Now if they can easily find it at home, what purpose is there in travelling to get it elsewhere? And this reason counts even more, the less the people are devoted to their pleasures. So an abundance of goods is not enough in itself to draw large numbers of people together; some other cause beyond this is required to unite them in one place, and that is the ease and convenience of transport.

---

21 Piedmont was occupied by French and Spanish armies between 1536 and 1559, during Botero's boyhood.

## *10. On Convenience for Transport*

This convenience is provided either by land or by water. If the land is level it permits the easy transport of goods and merchandise of every sort on carts, horses, mules and other beasts of burden, and allows people to travel comfortably on foot, on horseback, in carriages, or in other ways. The Portuguese report that in some very broad plains in China they use coaches with sails, which someone attempted not many years ago in Spain.

Transport by water, if it is navigable, is incomparably better than transport by land, both for facility and speed, because incomparably bigger cargoes are transported from very distant lands by water than by land, in less time, at lower cost and with less effort. Now navigable waters consist of rivers, lakes and the sea, which are natural waterways, or of canals and lakes constructed by human labour and skill, as was Lake Moeris in Egypt, which measured four hundred and fifty miles around. In truth it seems that God created water not merely as an element necessary for the perfection of nature, but even more as a most convenient way to transport goods from one place to another. For since it is His Divine Majesty's will that human beings should embrace one another, as members of a single body, He shared out His blessings in such a way that no single country received everything, in order that communication would arise between those who needed the goods of others, who similarly needed goods from them, which would give rise to communication, and out of this communication, love would arise, and out of love, unity. To facilitate communication He created water, of such nature and substance that through its density it is able to support the heaviest burdens, and by its liquidity to convey them wherever one wishes, with the aid of the winds or oars. In this way East is connected to West, and South to North, so that one can say that what is produced in one place, because of the ease with which it can be obtained, is produced everywhere.

Now the sea is without doubt of greater service than lakes or rivers, by reason of its almost limitless expanse and the consistency of its water, but the sea is of little use unless you have a capacious, safe harbour; by capacious I mean in its extent, and in the depth of water at its entrance, middle, and extremities; by safe I mean protected from all or many of the winds, or at least from the stormiest. Of all the winds, it is said that the northerly is the most easily borne, and that when the northeast wind tosses the sea, it becomes calm as soon as the wind abates; but southerly winds roil and agitate it to such a degree, as the Gulf of Venice proves beyond doubt, that even after the wind has died down it billows and rages for a long time. Now harbours will either be safe by their nature, like those of Messina or Marseille, or through skilful construction that imitates nature, like those of Genoa and Palermo.

Lakes are almost little seas, so that they too, depending on their size and other conveniences, are very useful to the local populations, as can be seen in New Spain, where the lake of Mexico, ninety miles in circumference, is ornamented with fifty big towns, among which is the great city of Tenochtitlán,[22] the metropolis of that immense realm.

Rivers too are very important, particularly those that follow lengthy courses through broad regions and very rich mercantile countries, like the Po in Italy, the Scheldt in Flanders, the Loire and the Seine in France, and the Danube and the Rhine in Germany. And just as lakes are like little copies made by nature of the bays and inlets of the sea, in the same way canals, through which the water of lakes and rivers flows, are models or as it were manmade imitations of rivers. The ancient kings of Egypt caused a canal to be made from the Nile to the city of Heroopolis,[23] and tried to construct another one from the Red Sea to the Mediterranean, to join our sea to the Indian Ocean, so as to facilitate

22 Today Mexico City.
23 Today Suez.

the transport of goods and enrich their kingdom. It is well known how many attempts have been made to cut through the Isthmus of Corinth and link the Ionian Sea to the Aegean. One of the sultans of Cairo had a canal constructed from the river Euphrates to Aleppo. Around Bruges and Ghent and in other places in Flanders one can see many canals that have been skilfully constructed, at incalculable cost, but of much greater value in facilitating commerce and the movement of people. In Lombardy many cities have wisely secured this facility for themselves, but none more so than Milan, which draws to itself water from the river Ticino and Lake Maggiore, by means of a canal that matches the grandeur of ancient Rome. In this way it enriches itself with endless merchandise, while another canal draws water from the river Adda to bring home the fruits and produce of its very bountiful territory; and it would be even better served if the canals of Pavia and Ivrea were cleaned out.

Now with respect to canals and rivers, their value for trade and transport depends not only on their length, as we have said, but also on their depth, their placidity, the consistency of their water, and their breadth. Depth is important because deep waters bear heavier loads, and navigation is without risk; placidity, because it makes travelling in either direction easier; some hold that those who designed the canal that runs from the Ticino to Milan erred, for because of its steep gradient and the impetus this gives to the water, it has a very swift current, which makes navigation upstream extremely laborious and time-consuming. Concerning rivers, nature has dealt very kindly with Gallia Celtica and Gallia Belgica,[24] for the rivers of the former are mostly very calm and placid, so that navigation in both directions is incredibly easy, because many of these rivers originate in flat plains, so that their course is not precipitous. They do not flow through mountains, not even for a short distance, but flow for many hundreds of miles through very

---

24   The Roman names for central and northern France.

extensive plains, in which (as if at play) they meander now one way, now another, and as they advance and retreat like this they favour many cities with their water and their service. But no country in Europe is better provided with rivers than the region of Belgium that is commonly called Flanders. Here the Scheldt, the Meuse, the Moselle, the Niers, the Roer and the Rhine, which divides into three enormous branches, flow placidly and in a straight course across the province, and enrich it with immense wealth thanks to the ease of navigation and trade.

This is certainly lacking in Italy, because the country is long, narrow and bisected by the Apennines, so that its rivers are short and cannot grow very much in size or moderate their violent currents. Almost all the rivers of Lombardy originate either in the Alps, like the Ticino, the Adda, the Lambro, the Serio, and the Adige, or in the Apennines, like the Taro, the Lenza, the Panaro and the Reno. And after only a short distance, during which they deserve to be called torrents rather than rivers, they reach the Po as it makes its journey between the Alps and the Apennines. It is therefore the only river that is navigable, because by traversing the entire length of the region it has room to grow bigger and enrich itself with the aid of its many tributaries, and moderate its natural impetus by reason of its lengthy course. Nevertheless, because the tributaries with their short courses enter the Po with great violence, they swell and speed it up as they do, making it dangerous to the cities, even the strongest ones, and also to the countryside. But the rivers of Romagna and the other parts of Italy flow down as raging torrents from one slope or the other of the Apennines, quickly reaching the Adriatic or the Ionian or the Tyrrhenian seas, so that most of them do not have enough space to reduce their velocity, and none has sufficient time to grow broad enough to be navigable, for those brief stretches of the Arno or the Tiber that are navigable are scarcely worth mentioning.

The density of the water is important too, for nobody can deny that one river's water bears loads better than another's. When the obelisk that now stands in the piazza in front of St Peter's in Rome was erected under Pope Sixtus V, it was recognized by experience that the water of the Tiber was stronger and more resistant than the water of the Nile.[25] The Seine, a medium-sized river in France, bears ships of such size and supports such heavy loads that those who do not see it will not believe it. There is no river in the world that can sustain such weight in proportion to its size, so that even though it is of only middling size it wonderfully supplies the needs of Paris, a city that in population and abundance of all manner of goods far surpasses every other in Christendom.

Here someone could well ask me how one kind of water can carry more than another. Some say that this is due to its earthy quality, which makes it denser, and thus firm and solid. The only objection to this argument is the Nile, whose water is so full of earth and silt that in the Scriptures it is called a turbid river,[26] and which cannot be drunk unless it has been thoroughly purged in cisterns. It not only irrigates and softens the soil of Egypt with its liquidity, but even more, it fertilizes and as it were manures it with its richness, yet it is not one of the strongest rivers for carrying ships and loads. From this I would think that to explain this one should not examine the earthy thickness of the water, but rather a certain kind of viscosity that binds it together and condenses it, making it better able to support and bear loads. But where does this quality come from? From two things: first, if a river rises and

---

25   This obelisk was originally brought from Egypt under the Emperor Caligula and was erected in the Circus he built on the Vatican Hill. St Peter was supposedly martyred there. The obelisk was moved a short distance from there, and re-erected on the site where it now stands in front of St Peter's basilica, under the direction of the architect Domenico Fontana in 1586, while Botero was living in Rome. See the description in his *Della trasportatione dell'obelisco vaticano et delle fabriche di nostro signore papa Sisto V fatte dal cavallier Domenico Fontana. Libro primo* (Rome: D. Basa, 1590). How Botero could have inferred a difference in density between the waters of the two rivers from the relocation of the obelisk is not clear, because it was not transported on either of them.

26   Joshua XIII, 3.

flows through soft, rich lands; because rivers share the nature of the earth that forms their beds and banks, they too become rich, with a quality like oil. Then the brevity and slowness of a river's course are significant too, because a lengthy course and swift current thin out the water's substance and break up its viscosity. This is what happens to the Nile, which runs almost two thousand miles as the crow flies, and far more, indirectly; it falls from extremely steep, rocky places, where the impetuosity of the water, its momentum, and the extraordinary speed with which it falls, turn it into almost a very fine rain, making its waters so thin and tired that they lose all their viscous properties. The rivers of Germany and France retain all their viscosity because they rise and flow through rich, pleasant countries, and are usually not violent or fast flowing. The water of the Seine proves that this is the true reason, for when you use it to wash your hands, it clings to you like soap and cleans you marvellously of every stain.

But let us consider a river's breadth. This is necessary in the rivers and canals of which we have spoken, so that boats can manoeuvre conveniently, turn in all directions, and allow space for one another. But a river's breadth alone, without depth, does not serve our purpose because it disperses and spreads the water out, making it useless for navigation, as with the Rio de la Plata, which because of its enormous width has an uneven bed, is mostly shallow, and is full of rocks and little islands. For the same reason the rivers in Spain are barely navigable because indeed they have wide beds, but they are spread out, shifting and uneven. And this is enough to say about rivers.

Now because water is so useful in so many ways for the greatness of cities, those cities that enjoy access to several kinds of navigable water are the best situated, like those that have a port that is suitable for various kinds of traffic, or a lake or a river. To some it may now seem we have discovered that the real foundation, or rather consummation of a city's greatness is ease of transportation. But this is not so: something more than that is required to attract people and make them gather in one place rather than another. Where communication is not easy there cannot be many people, as we can certainly learn from the mountains, where we see many castles and hamlets, but no population that can be called numerous. The reason is that these places are located in such rugged sites that the things useful and necessary for civilized life can be conveyed there only with enormous toil and trouble. For this reason and no other, Fiesole is empty and Florence is full of people, for the former is situated in too steep a place, the latter in the plain. And in Rome we see how people have abandoned the Aventine and the other hills, and moved to the lowlands close to the Tiber, because of the facility that the flat land and the water provide for trade and the movement of goods.

But where communications are easy one does not automatically see a notable city. Undoubtedly Messina has a far better harbour than Naples, but nonetheless, if you look to the population, Naples makes more than two Messinas. The port of Cartagena is superior to that of Genoa in every respect, but Genoa surpasses Cartagena in wealth and population, and everything else. What harbour is more beautiful, more secure and more capacious than the bay of Cattaro?[27] Yet no city worthy of note has ever stood there.

What shall we say of rivers? It is said (an astounding thing) that the Marañon[28] in Peru runs for six thousand miles, and has a mouth more than sixty miles wide, and there is the Rio de la Plata, which carries a much greater volume of water though it is not as long, and is said to have an estuary one-hundred and fifty miles across. In New France there is the River Canada,[29] which is more than thirty-five miles wide and two hundred fathoms deep at its mouth. Africa too has enormous rivers, the Senegal, the Gambia, and the Cuanza, recently discovered in the great Kingdom

---

27    Kotor in Montenegro.
28    The Amazon.
29    The St Lawrence.

of Angola, whose mouth is estimated to be thirty-five miles in breadth, without any significant population. On the contrary: those savages who inhabit its banks live in caves and hollow trees in the company of crustaceans, with whom they live safely and on very friendly terms.[30] In Asia the Menan[31] (which in the language of those people means Mother of Waters), the Mekong, which is navigable for over two thousand miles, the Indus, and the other royal rivers are all thickly populated; nonetheless the Ob, which is the greatest of them all, attaining a breadth of over eighty miles where it enters the Scythian Ocean[32] (which leads some to think it may be the way by which the Caspian Sea empties itself into the ocean), is without a single famous city.

Finally, if ease of communication is the consummation of a city's greatness, why is it that along the banks of the same river, where communication is equally easy, one city is greater than another? Without doubt, the easy transport of goods is not sufficient: some attractive power is needed besides that, which will draw and direct traffic to one place rather than another.

---

30  This curious detail opens a small window into the types of sources Botero used, and
    how he used them. Its wording is very close to the last paragraph of a letter writ-
    ten by the Portuguese Jesuit Baltasar Barreira to Father Sebastião de Morais, from
    Luanda, 31 Jan. 1582, in Antonio Brásio, ed., *Monumenta missionaria Africana. África
    ocidental (1570–1599)*, vol. 3: 211. The original reads: "Ao longo deste Rio me espantei
    de ver huã sorte de gente que tẽ suas casas e habitaõ debaixo das raízes dos manues,
    que são arvores do Rio, que lanção as raízes dos ramos para baixo, onde vivem tam
    acompanhados de caranguejos, que já os não estranhaõ, porque, quando comẽ lhe
    andão por cimar do comer, e quando dorme por cima dos olhos." [Along the river-
    bank I was surprised to see a people who have houses and live under the mangrove
    roots – river trees whose branches root downwards – in the company of so many
    crabs that they do not find it strange, because when they eat, the crabs crawl over
    their food, and when they sleep, over their eyes]. De Morais (1534–88) was confessor
    to the Infanta Margarita, princess of Parma, from 1565 until her death in 1578, dur-
    ing which time he also served as vice-rector of Carlo Borromeo's newly founded Je-
    suit college of the Brera in Milan, where he may well have met Botero, who was there
    in 1571–2 and again in 1577. He returned to Portugal as Jesuit provincial in 1580, was
    appointed first bishop of Japan in 1587, and died en route there off the coast of Mo-
    zambique a year later.
31  The Mae Nam Chao Phraya in Thailand.
32  The Arctic Sea.

# BOOK II

## *I.*

So far we have discussed the suitability of our city's site, the fertility of its land, and the ease of its communications. Now let us look for the things that induce people – by their nature indifferent to whether they live here or there – to move, and for goods to be transported to one place rather than another. Let us speak first of the particular methods the Romans employed for this purpose, and then of the methods common to them and to others.

## 2. *On the Particular Methods Employed by the Romans*

The first method was to grant sanctuary and citizenship, as Romulus did, so that Rome's population would increase because of the security that prevailed there, at a time when the neighbouring towns were oppressed by tyrants and the nearby lands were consequently full of bandits. Nor was he mistaken, for a great many men who had no homes or were living precariously in their own countries flocked there. Then because the women needed for procreation were lacking, Romulus announced that certain festivals would be celebrated in a very grand manner, and seized most of the young women who attended these festivals, so it is no wonder that men of an almost iron temperament were born from such fierce people. In our own day Geneva has increased in a similar way, though in a far more licentious and detestable manner, because after rebelling against its legitimate sovereign and breaking away from the Catholic Church and Christ Himself, it has made itself a den and retreat for apostates and people who, unwilling to live peaceably in their own countries, have repaired to this refuge and made it their nesting place.[1] And not long ago Casimir, one of

---

1 Geneva revolted against its ruling prince-bishop and adopted the Reformed religion under Calvin's leadership in 1536.

the Rhenish counts-palatine, also sheltered all sorts of people and heresies and founded a city of considerable size, where there is a collection of every kind of apostasy and a flood of every impiety.[2] And for this reason it is just a gathering place like Geneva, unworthy to be celebrated by us among cities.

In order to populate Porto Ferraio, Grand-Duke Cosimo of Tuscany confined bandits in surety there and banished many who deserved exile for some crime to that place,[3] and Grand-Duke Francesco his son followed his example to build up the population of Pisa and Livorno. But as we said before, force and necessity are not good ways to attract inhabitants and make a city grow, because people who are constrained to stay in one place are like seeds cast upon the sand, where they never put down roots. But let us return to the subject of sanctuary. There can be no denying that moderate freedom and legitimate privileges are of great help in populating a place, and for this reason, other things being equal, free cities are usually more famous and better populated than those that are subject to princes and monarchs.

The second means by which Rome grew was by extending citizenship and magistracies to the well-deserving places they called "free towns" (municipia), since the honour of being citizens of Rome and the very extensive privileges attached to citizenship induced all those bound by party loyalties, or favours, or services performed for the republic, to settle in the city, where they could hope for an office or a magistracy, and those who did not aim so high could at least use their votes on behalf of a relative, a friend, or a patron who was seeking office. In this way Rome became

---

2   The Calvinist Count-Palatine Johann Casimir founded a Reformed university, the Casimirium, at Neustadt an der Haardt in 1578. It only lasted until 1583, when he moved to Heidelberg as regent for his nephew, the young Elector Frederick.

3   Portoferraio, the chief town on the island of Elba, was refounded and fortified by Duke Cosimo I in the mid-sixteenth century. Cf the letter of Claudio Tolomei to Agostino de' Landi (14 Nov. 1544) with a project for the new town, in Paola Barocchi, ed., Scritti d'arte del Cinquecento , vol. 3: 3123–30.

populous and was enriched by the influx of an infinite number of noble and wealthy people who, either individually or collectively, were honoured with Roman citizenship.

The third means was the perpetual delight Rome afforded the curious, which is to say the great number of marvellous things that were done there: the triumphs of victorious generals, wonderful buildings, mock naval combats, gladiatorial contests, hunting of wild beasts, public banquets, the Apollonian and Secular Games,[4] and others, which were celebrated with unbelievable pomp and ceremony, and all the other suchlike things that drew the curious to Rome. And because these attractions were almost continuous, Rome was almost always full of foreigners.

## 3. On Colonies

What shall we say about colonies? Did they contribute to Rome's greatness, or not? It cannot be doubted that they aided in the growth of Rome's power, but that they may also have increased the number of its inhabitants is highly debatable. I think however that they were extremely beneficial because, although some would argue that by sending out people to its colonies Rome reduced rather than increased its population, nevertheless the opposite may have occurred. This is because, just as plants cannot grow and multiply as well in the nursery where they are sown as in the open ground where they are transplanted, in the same way human beings do not propagate as successfully when enclosed within the walls of the city where they are born, as they would in different places to which they are sent, because either the plague or some contagious disease devours them, or famine and hunger force them to seek another dwelling-place, or foreign wars kill off

---

4   A religious festival celebrated every hundred years.

the bravest among them while civil conflicts uproot the peaceful ones from their homes, and poverty and scarcity deprive many of the desire and the means to marry and have children. Now the people who would have died in Rome for these reasons, or would have dispersed, or would not have set up households and left descendants, escaped these dangers when they were moved to other places. Established in colonies, with houses and land, they were assured of taking wives and having children, and in this way they multiplied immeasurably, and from ten became a hundred.

But someone will say: what does this matter? Let us suppose that those who were sent to the colonies would not help their fatherland to grow if they remained in their homes: how then will they do this by leaving? First, because the colonies and the mother city form as it were a single body, and then because love of the fatherland and dependency on it (which can be strengthened in several ways), and the hope and desire for advancement in honours and wealth, will always attract the noblest and wealthiest persons, so that the city will become richer and more populous. Who will deny that the thirty colonies that issued from Alba Longa, as from a root-stock, or the many colonies sent forth by Rome, did not bring magnificence and greatness to both of these cities? And that the Portuguese who have left Lisbon to live and farm the land in the Azores, Cape Verde, Madeira and the other islands have increased Lisbon much more than if they had not departed? It is true that if colonies are to cause their mother city to grow they must be close at hand, for otherwise distance cools affection and cuts off communication, which is why for six hundred years the Romans established no colonies outside Italy; the first outside Italy were Carthage and Narbonne, as was said at length in *The Reason of State*, in the chapter on colonies.[5]

---

5   Book VI, chapter 4.

These are the particular and most effective means by which the Romans drew people to their cities. Now let us speak of the methods employed commonly by them and other peoples, and it will not be out of place for us to begin with religion, which must be the guiding principle of all our actions.

## *4. On Religion*

Religion and the worship of God are so necessary and so important that they infallibly draw to themselves the majority of human beings and their affairs, and those cities that have renown and authority over others in this are also favoured with greatness. According to Pliny, Jerusalem was among the chief cities of the East, chiefly because of religion, of which it was the capital city, besides being the capital of the kingdom. The high priests, priests and Levites resided there; offerings and sacrifices were made there, and vows sworn to God; three times every year almost the entire people gathered there, so that Josephus recounts that when Titus Vespasian laid siege to the city it contained two and one-half million people, which is an amazing, not to say incredible thing, especially since the city's walls were only four miles around; but it was written by a person who would have known, and who had no reason to lie.[6] Jeroboam, after he was elected king of Israel, knowing that his subjects could not live without religious observances and sacrifices, and that if they went to sacrifice at Jerusalem it would be easy for them to reunite there with the tribe of Judah and the House of David, therefore banished religion from his kingdom and introduced idolatry. He caused two golden calves to be made and set up at the outermost points of his kingdom, and enjoined the people: "Nolite ultra ascendere in Hierusalem;

---

6   Titus, the son of the emperor Vespasian and future emperor, besieged and conquered
    Jerusalem in 70 CE.

ecce dii tui, Israel, qui te eduxerunt de terra Aegypti."[7] Religion has such power to increase cities and expand kingdoms, and possesses such force of attraction, that in order not to yield to his rival in attracting and maintaining factions, Jeroboam impiously introduced idolatry into the place of true religion. He was the first who openly trampled the law and the respect due to God, in order to reign, giving an example for others to follow, truly a thing that is no less foolish than impious.

Those who make a show of prudence and reason of state, as they call it, think that human reason serves better than divine reason for maintaining subjects in obedience to their princes, and that the cogitations of I know not what miserable worms serve better than the favour of His Divine Majesty. Such men are the ruin of kings, a plague on kingdoms, a scandal to Christianity, the sworn enemies of the Church, or rather of God, against Whom, imitating the giants of old, they build a new Tower of Babel, which in the end will bring forth only confusion and ruin for them: "Qui habitat in coelis irridebit eos et Dominus subsannabit eos."[8] Hear, princes, what the prophet Isaiah says of the counsellors of Pharaoh: "Sapientes consiliarii Pharaonis dederunt consilium insipiens ... deceperunt Aegyptum angulum populorum eius. Dominus miscuit in medio eius spiritum vertiginis, et errare fecerunt Aegyptum in omni opere suo, sicut ebrius et vomens."[9] If this were the proper place I would easily demonstrate that the overthrow of kingdoms and the destruction of Christian princes spring mainly from this accursed notion, by which we have disarmed ourselves

---

7   III Kings, XII, 28: "Go up no more to Jerusalem: Behold thy gods, O Israel, who brought thee out of the land of Egypt."

8   Ps. II, 4: "He that dwelleth in heaven shall laugh at them; and the Lord shall deride them."

9   Isaiah XIX, 11, 13–14: "The wise counsellors of Pharaoh have given foolish counsel ... they have deceived Egypt, the stay of the people thereof. The Lord hath mingled in the midst thereof the spirit of giddiness: and they have caused Egypt to err in all its works, as a drunken man staggereth and vomiteth."

and deprived ourselves of God's blessings and protection, and placed the weapons and the scourge of divine justice in the hands of the Turks and the Calvinists, against ourselves. But let it suffice for now to admonish those princes who follow the doctrine of reason of state which tramples on God's law, that they should learn from their teacher Jeroboam, whose works they imitate, and should fear the fate that befell him: to avenge his impiety, against his son Nadab God raised up King Baasha, who slew him and all his progeny: "Non dimisit ne unam quidem animam de semine eius, donec deleret eum."[10] But let us return to what we were saying.

The power of religion to increase the population of a place, through the possession of a famous relic, some notable sign of divine assistance, or some authority in ecclesiastical governance, can be clearly seen from the examples of Loreto in Italy, Mont Saint-Michel in France, Guadalupe, Montserrat and Santiago de Compostela in Spain, and so many other places which, though lonely and desolate, rocky and forbidding, are daily frequented by infinite multitudes who flock to them from far distant countries, impelled by nothing but their fervour and piety, in spite of the devil and his allies the Huguenots. This is no wonder, for there is nothing more efficacious to move the hearts of men and draw them to itself than God, the supreme good. He is constantly desired and sought after, as the ultimate end, by all things animate and inanimate. Light bodies seek Him in the heights, heavy ones in the centre of the Earth, the heavens seek Him by circling in their orbits, plants by flowering, trees by bearing fruit, animals by reproducing their kind, men by seeking happiness and peace of mind. But because God is by His nature so hidden that human senses cannot reach Him, and so refulgent that the human intellect cannot bear it, everyone turns to where He leaves some trace

---

10   III Kings XV, 29: "He left not so much as one soul of his seed, till he had utterly destroyed him."

of His power or reveals some sign of His beneficence, as was usually seen, and is to be seen, in the mountains or the deserts.

Does not Rome owe its greatness to the blood of the martyrs and the relics of the saints, to the sanctity of its holy places, and its supreme authority over benefices and in questions of faith? Would not Rome be a desert, a solitude, if the holiness of its sacred places did not draw infinite numbers of people to it from the furthermost regions of the world, and if the apostolic throne and the power of the keys did not cause innumerable multitudes of people who have need of them to flock there? Milan, such an important city, will forever bear witness to the splendour and increase conferred on it by the piety and holiness of the great Cardinal Borromeo.[11] Princes came from the uttermost frontiers of the North to visit him, prelates journeyed from every region to seek his advice on their affairs, secular and regular clergy of every nation held Milan to be their homeland, the house of this saintly man their safe haven, his generosity their support, his life the most shining mirror of ecclesiastical discipline. It would be a lengthy matter to describe the magnificence with which he celebrated diocesan synods every year, and provincial synods every third year; how many new churches he built, how many old ones he reconstructed, how many he decorated and beautified; how many congregations he founded for men and women,[12] how many well-ordered colleges for the young, how many seminaries for the clergy; how many kinds of academies he created and founded for the inestimable benefit of his people; and how many commissions he gave to craftsmen and the guilds. And I would never finish, were I to recount the ways in which he enlarged the city of Milan and doubled the concourse of its people by fostering religious observances and divine worship.

---

11   Carlo Borromeo (1538–84), archbishop of Milan from 1560, canonized 1610.
12   Botero was a member of one of these, the Oblati di Sant'Ambrogio.

## 5. *On Universities*

Access to a seat of learning is of no little effect in attracting people, especially young men, to the city whose greatness we are discussing, for there are two ways by which persons of intelligence
and valour rise to honour and reputation: one is the career of
arms, the other that of letters, the former pursued on the field of
battle with lance and sword, the latter in the academy with books
and pen. Because men will greatly exert themselves for honour
or profit, and because some sciences bring a man certain wealth
and others lead to high rank, it is of no small importance that our
city have an academy or university, such that young men eager to
acquire virtue and learning will choose to attend it, rather than
some other one. This they will do if, besides having access to facili-
ties and teachers, they will enjoy the proper privileges and free-
doms; not those that give them licence to wallow with impunity
in every vice, but which provide a reasonable liberty in which they
can cheerfully and comfortably pursue their studies. (Since study
demands great toil and effort of both body and mind, the An-
cients called the goddess of learning Minerva, because the effort
of speculation saps the strength and weakens the nerves, and the
weariness of the body affects the mind, bringing forth melancholy
and sadness).[13] So it is fitting that the students be granted all the
privileges necessary to keep them happy and contented, but not
dissolute, as in the academies in Italy. There pens are transformed
into daggers and inkwells into gunpowder flasks, disputations into
bloody brawls, lecture halls into tournament yards, and students
into swordsmen. There uprightness is scorned and modesty is
held in disrepute, so that a young man who wishes to comport

---

13   A false etymology: partly following Cicero, *De natura deorum*, III, 24, Botero derives
     the name of Minerva from the Latin "qui minuit nervos" = "who weakens the nerves
     or sinews."

himself decorously is hard put to avoid ruin. But let us be done with these complaints.

An academy cannot flourish unless weapons and gambling are banned. King Francis I of France set aside a wide meadow close to the city of Paris and the river for the university students, who in his time were almost infinite in number, to take the air at their ease, pursue innocent diversions, and disport themselves as they pleased. There they wrestle, play at the barrier, at football and handball, at pall-mall, at leaping and running, with such joy as to delight not only themselves but the onlookers too; and in the mean time card games, dice, and the clash of arms all cease.

For these reasons it is most important that the city where you wish to found a university should enjoy good air, and a cheerful and beautiful site, where there would be rivers, springs and woods, for these things are very suitable for enticing the students. Such were Athens and Rhodes in ancient times, where learning conspicuously flourished. Galeazzo Visconti,[14] wishing to make Pavia famous and populous in addition to these attractions, was the first who forbade his subjects to go and study elsewhere, on pain of dire punishment. Since then other Italian princes have imitated him, but this method is fraught with distrust. There are honourable and generous ways to keep subjects within the state, and also to attract foreigners, by allowing them to pursue virtuous pastimes, ensuring an abundant supply of foodstuffs for them, upholding their privileges, offering them the opportunity to win renown in literary exercises, granting recognition to fine minds and rewarding them with prizes, and above all by bringing in teachers of great fame and reputation, like those whose lecture halls the great Pompey did not consider it beneath himself to frequent, when, after conquering all the Orient, he attended the schools of Rhodes. For a much higher reason Sigismund, king of Poland,[15]

---

14  Botero presumably refers to Giangaleazzo Visconti (1351–1402), duke of Milan from 1395.
15  Sigismund II Jagiello, reigned 1548–72.

barred his subjects from going abroad to study, as did the Catholic King[16] some years ago, so that they would not become infected with the heresies that appeared during Sigismund's reign, and that have reached their peak throughout the northern countries in our own time.

## 6. On Courts of Justice

Because charity and loving kindness are everywhere lacking, while the violence and greed of evil men are increasing, our lives, honour and wealth are all in the hands of the judges, and if they do not protect us against such men, our affairs will go badly. For this reason cities which have royal audiences, senates, parliaments, and all the other types of high courts are of necessity much frequented, both by the crowds of people seeking justice and by those who administer it, which requires many people: presidents, senators, advocates, procurators, solicitors, notaries, and other such persons. And most important of all, justice today is done only in return for ready money; nothing moves men more than the flow of money, and a magnet does not attract iron as powerfully as gold turns men's eyes and minds this way and that; the reason is that gold potentially contains within itself every kind of greatness, comfort and earthly good, so that one may say that those who possess it, possess everything that is to be had in this world. Now because of the great quantity of money that the administration of justice brings with it, capital cities, if they cannot claim jurisdiction in all civil and criminal cases, at least reserve to themselves the weightiest cases and appeals. This is certainly done for reasons of state, whose principal element is judicial authority, by which we hold dominion over the lives and property of every subject, but which is also a profitable matter, as we have noted. This is true everywhere, but much more where legal procedure is

16   Philip II of Spain.

based on Roman law, which is lengthier and requires more officials than the other legal systems. In England and Scotland, but above all in Turkey, where justice is rendered summarily, or as it were immediately, little benefit accrues to a city through the administration of justice, because cases will be decided in a single afternoon on the direct testimony of witnesses, lawsuits will be settled, and the weightiest cases will be speedily terminated. Extensions and prorogations, legal instruments and procedural devices, officials and intermediaries have no place there, for a decision is reached in a few quick strokes, so that the time, the expense, and the number of people involved are far less than Roman law requires. I do not mean to say however that sentencing should be prolonged or disputes should drag on interminably, for alas, they do go on far too long; in judicial matters delay is a form of injustice, for which solicitude and care to avoid errors are no excuse. So it is very important that justice be administered in our city, and that the highest court should have its seat there.

## 7. On Industry[17]

Nothing is more important for causing a state to grow, and for making it populous and well supplied with everything, than industry and a great number of crafts, some of which are essential, some beneficial to civil life, others desirable for display and show, yet others for the delight and entertainment of leisured persons. From this comes a flow of money and people, who are workers, or

---

17   This chapter occupied this place in the original edition of *Delle cause* in 1588, but in 1589 Botero incorporated it into *Della ragion di Stato*, replacing it in *Delle cause* with this note: "Because we said enough about industry when we were discussing the formation of states in Book VIII of *The Reason of State*, we refer the reader to that chapter." It remained as chapter 3 of Book VIII in subsequent editions of *Della ragion di Stato*, except for the 1590 Rome edition, where it appears in both places. Peterson includes both the note and the chapter in his translation; Hawkins translates only the chapter itself.

who deal in the finished goods, or who supply the workers with materials, or who buy, sell and transport the ingenious products of human hands and minds from one place to another.

To ennoble Constantinople and increase its population, Selim I,[18] emperor of the Turks, had several thousand excellent workers transferred there from the royal city of Tauris,[19] and later from great Cairo. The Polish people too understood this well, for when they elected Henri, duke of Anjou, to be their king, one of the things they required of him was that he should bring a hundred families of artisans to their country.[20]

Now since human ingenuity competes with nature, someone will ask me which is of greater value for improving a place and increasing its population: the fertility of its soil, or the industry of its people? The answer is undoubtedly industry, first of all because the things made by skilled human hands are far more numerous and costly than those produced by nature, for nature furnishes the material and the subject, but human skill and cleverness impart to them their inexpressible variety of forms. Wool is a crude, simple product of nature, but how beautiful, manifold and varied are the things that human skill creates from it? How many and how great are the profits that result from the labour of those who card it, spin, warp and weave it, dye, shear and stitch it, shape it in a thousand ways, and transport it from one place to another. Silk too is a simple product of nature, but how great a variety of beautiful fabrics are created from it by human skill, which makes the filthy secretion of a lowly caterpillar into something prized by princes and esteemed by queens, and finally sought after by everyone for adornment.

Moreover, far more people make their living from manufacturing than from their revenues, as many Italian cities attest, but

---

18  Reigned 1512–20.
19  Tabriz in Persia.
20  He was elected in 1573 but never crowned; in 1574 he returned to France to assume the throne as Henri III on the death of his brother Charles IX.

chiefly Venice, Florence, Genoa and Milan, of whose greatness and magnificence there is no need to speak, and where the wool and silk industries support almost two-thirds of the inhabitants. And if we pass from cities to countries, those who have carefully calculated the resources of France tell us that its revenues amount to more than fifteen million *scudi* a year, and the same people affirm that it has a population of more than fifteen million souls. But let us assume that they are no more than fifteen million; this would mean one *scudo* of revenues per head, so therefore all the other wealth comes from industry. But who does not see that this is so of everything? The revenues from iron mines are not very big, but an infinite number of people make their living from working the iron and trading in it; they mine it, refine it and smelt it, they sell it wholesale and retail, they make it into engines of war and weapons for attack and defence, into endless kinds of tools for farming, building and every craft, and for the everyday needs and innumerable necessities of life, for which iron is no less needful than bread. So if we compare the income that the mine owners get from their iron, with the profits that the artisans and merchants draw from it through their industriousness, which also enriches princes to an incredible degree through the payment of customs duties, we should find that industry far outstrips nature.

Compare marble with the statues, colossi, columns, friezes and the infinite number of works that are made from it; compare timber with the galleys, galleons, ships and the endless types of other vessels, warships, merchantmen and pleasure-craft, or the statues, household furniture and innumerable other articles that are made from it with plane, chisel and lathe; compare artists' pigments with their paintings, and set the price of the latter against the value of the former (the most excellent painter Zeuxis gave away his pictures for nothing, observing generously that they could not be bought at any price), and you will understand how the finished work is worth far more than the raw material, and how many more people live by their crafts than from the fruits of nature.

The power of industry is such that there is no silver mine or gold mine in New Spain and Peru that can be compared to it, and the duties on the commerce of Milan are worth more to the Catholic King than the mines of Zacatecas and Jalisco. Italy is a country in which, as I said before, there are no significant silver or gold mines, and nor are there in France, yet even so both countries abound in money and treasure thanks to their industries. Flanders too has no veins of metals, but nonetheless, thanks to the enormous variety of wonderful works that were made there with indescribable skill and craftsmanship, while the country was still at peace, it had no reason to envy the wealth of the mines in Hungary and Transylvania, nor was there any country in Europe that was more splendid, more wealthy and more thickly populated; nor was there any country in Europe, or the whole world, where there were so many great cities so frequented by foreigners. So because of the incomparable treasure that the Emperor Charles V drew from this country, some justly called it His Majesty's Indies. Nature confers form on primary substance, and from natural material human ingenuity creates an endless number of artificial objects, because nature is to the craftsman what the primary material is to the natural agent.

Therefore a prince who wishes his city to be well populated must establish all kinds of crafts and industries there, which he can do by bringing in skilled artisans from other countries and giving them suitable workplaces and lodgings, by taking note of ingenious minds and appreciating the rare and singular inventions they devise, and by offering prizes for perfection and excellence. But above all he must not permit the export of raw materials from his state, whether wool, silk, timber, metals or any other such thing, because skilled craftsmen will depart along with them, and the trade in manufactured goods supports a far greater number of people than the traffic in raw materials. The prince's revenues from the export of finished goods are much greater than from that of primary materials; for example velvet brings in more revenue than raw silk, serge[21] more than raw wool, linen more than flax, ropes more than hemp. Taking account of this, in recent years the kings of France and England have forbidden the export of wool from their kingdoms, as the Catholic King later did too. But these prohibitions could not be obeyed at once, because those countries abound in such incredible quantities of very fine wool that there were not enough skilled workers to use all of it. Although these princes perhaps did this because the profit and the customs revenue from woollen cloth are much higher than those from raw wool, nevertheless this is also the way to increase the population of a country, because many more people live from the manufacture of cloth than from the production of raw wool; and from this comes the wealth and grandeur of the king, because a numerous population is what makes the land fertile, and by means of its skills and its hands endows raw materials with a thousand forms.

## 8. On Fiscal Privileges

In this our present century the people are taxed so heavily by their rulers, who are driven partly by greed and partly by necessity, that they eagerly go wherever they discover the slightest hope of fiscal immunity or franchise, as witness the fairs, which attract vast numbers of merchants and common folk for the sole reason that they are free of tariffs and impositions. In our own time the royal city of Naples has grown significantly in both population and buildings because of the tax exemptions and franchises granted to its inhabitants, and it would have grown still more if the Catholic King had not strictly forbidden further building, in response to the complaints and protests of the barons, whose lands were being emptied of people, or for some other reason.

---

21   "Rascie" in the original: a general term for rough woollen cloth.

The cities of Flanders were the most mercantile and the most frequented in all of Europe, and if you seek for the reason, you will see that it is, among other things, their freedom from indirect taxation, because the merchandise that entered and left these cities (in immense quantities) paid hardly any duties. Then all those who have founded new cities have of necessity granted very broad fiscal immunities and privileges, at least to the earliest inhabitants, in order to attract people, and the same has been done to restore cities ravaged by the plague, or devastated by war, or smitten by other divine scourges. The plague that afflicted Italy for close to three years, described by Boccaccio,[22] was so cruel that between March and July it carried off almost a hundred thousand souls in Florence. It killed a similar number in Venice, leaving the city almost deserted, and so to repopulate it the Signoria issued a proclamation granting the right of citizenship to all who would move there with their families and remain for the space of two years. And on more than one occasion these same lords who govern Venice have averted a dire shortage of foodstuffs by promising freedom from taxes to those who brought provisions into the city.

## 9. On the Possession of Some Valuable Commodity

It will also be of great value in drawing people to our city if it should dispose of some prized commodity. This can happen if it is the only territory where this commodity is produced, or where it is produced in the greatest quantity, or where it is produced in an excellent form. Thus the Moluccas alone produce cloves, Sabaea alone produces incense, and Palestine or elsewhere produce balsam; Calicut produces the greatest quantity of pepper and Ceylon the most cinnamon; the best salt is produced in Cyprus, the

---

22  Beginning in 1348. It is described in the Introduction to Boccaccio's *Decameron*.

best sugar in Madeira, the best wool in a few towns in Spain and England. There are also excellent manufactures that flourish in one place rather than another, either because of the quality of the water, the cleverness of the inhabitants, some secret method they employ, or some similar reason, such as the weapons of Damascus and Shiraz, the tapestries of Arras, the serges of Florence, the velvets of Genoa, the brocades of Milan, the scarlet cloths of Venice. Here I should not fail to say that in China nearly every craft has attained perfection, for many reasons, but among them, because sons are required to practise the same trade as their fathers; they are born as it were with their minds set on their fathers' profession, and their fathers conceal nothing from them, but instruct them with great love, diligence, persistence and care, so that the craftsmen attain the highest degree of beauty and refinement that one could wish, as can be seen from those few works that are brought from China to the Philippines, from the Philippines to Mexico, and from Mexico to Seville. But let us return to our discussion.

Some other cities are mistresses of a particular trade, not because a commodity originates in their territory or is manufactured by their inhabitants, but because they have dominion over the neighbouring country or sea. In the former instance, the infinite riches of New Spain and Peru are all gathered into Seville because of its authority over those countries; in the latter case, through its control of the sea, Lisbon draws to itself the pepper of Cochin, the cinnamon of Ceylon and the other riches of India, which can be transported at sea only by itself or under its safe conduct. In almost the same way, ninety years ago Venice was almost the mistress of the trade in spices, for before the Portuguese took India they were conveyed through the Red Sea to Suez, then on camelback to Cairo and down the Nile to the great city of Alexandria, where they were purchased by the Venetians, who sent their great galleys there and distributed the spices to almost the whole of Europe at an enormous profit. Today almost all this trade has passed to Lisbon, where every year by a new route the Portuguese carry the spices they have taken out of the hands of the Moors and Turks, and then sell them to the Spaniards, the French, the English, and all the northern countries. This Indies trade is of such importance that on its own it is sufficient to enrich Portugal and make it abound in everything.

Some other cities dominate merchandise and commerce because they occupy a site that is convenient for many foreign nations, and that serves them as a warehouse or depository, like Malacca and Hormuz in the Orient; Alexandria and Constantinople, Messina and Genoa in the Mediterranean; Antwerp, Amsterdam, Danzig and Narva in the northern ocean; and Frankfurt and Nuremberg in Germany. Many important merchants establish their storehouses in these cities, to which the people of the nearby region go to obtain what they need, attracted by the convenience of transportation. And this consists of a safe, capacious harbour, convenient bays and inlets of the sea, navigable rivers that run through the cities or close by, lakes and canals, or let us say waterways, and safe, level roads. Speaking of roads, we should not fail to mention that over a long period of time the kings of Cusco (called in their language Incas) had two roads constructed, two thousand miles in length, and so pleasant and convenient, so straight and level, that they yield in no way to the grandeur of the Romans. Here you see very steep mountains levelled, very deep valleys filled in, fearsome crags cut away; the trees planted in rows on either side provide both shade for the travellers, and inexpressible delight from the singing of the birds that are always there. Nor is there a lack of inns well supplied with every necessity, or of palaces, which they build on hilltops, competing as it were in a joyful display of elegance, or delightful villas and pleasant countryside, with a thousand other beauties to satisfy both the eye with their variety and the mind with their wondrous effects, some due to nature, some to human handiwork.

But returning to our discussion, it will be very beneficial if the prince understands the natural advantages of the site, and works judiciously to improve it, for instance by protecting the harbour with breakwaters, facilitating the loading and unloading of cargoes, keeping the sea free of pirates, making the rivers navigable, building suitable warehouses big enough to contain large stocks of merchandise, straightening and repairing the roads, both over the plains and through the mountains. In this respect the kings of China deserve great praise, because at unbelievable cost they have paved all the roads in that most famous kingdom, built bridges of stone over gigantic rivers, cut down unbelievably tall, rugged mountains, and paved the lowlands with flagstones, so that one can travel on horseback or on foot as easily in winter as in summer, and transport goods without difficulty either on carts or pack-animals. Undoubtedly some Italian princes are very negligent in this matter; in their countries in wintertime horses drown and carriages sink in the mud, so that the transport of merchandise becomes extremely difficult, and journeys that should take a day can barely be completed in three or more. The roads in many parts of France are equally bad, in the provinces of Poitou, Saintonge, Beauce and Burgundy. But this is not the place to criticize such famous provinces, so let us pass on.

## 10. On Political Dominion

Political dominion is of the highest importance for making a place great, because it brings with it dependence, dependence brings gatherings of people, and the concourse of people brings greatness. Cities that have dominion and authority over others attract public wealth and private fortunes in various ways; here the ambassadors of foreign princes and the agents of the lesser towns congregate; the weightiest cases are argued, both civil and criminal, and appeals are referred; the affairs and negotiations of private persons and communities are debated by men of rank, and the state's revenues are collected and disbursed; here the wealthiest and most distinguished citizens of other places seek to establish

alliances and put down roots. All these things give rise to an abundance of money, a most powerful lure that attracts merchants
and artisans, workers and labourers of all sorts from the remotest
places. In this way the city steadily grows, in the magnificence of
its buildings, the size of its population, and the abundance of all
kinds of goods. It grows in proportion to its dominion, which is
demonstrated by all those cities that once had, or now have notable jurisdiction: Pisa, Siena, Genoa, Lucca, Florence and Brescia.
That city's territory measures a hundred miles in length and forty
in breadth, and contains not only the very fertile plain, but also
many important valleys, and many towns and castles with populations of more than a thousand households, making a total of almost three hundred and forty thousand people. Such in Germany
are many free and imperial cities like Nuremberg, Lübeck and
Augsburg; such was Ghent in Flanders, which used to muster a
hundred thousand fighting men when it raised its great banner. I
will not speak here of Sparta, Carthage, Athens, Rome and Venice,
whose greatness grew in proportion to their dominion, to such
a degree that – leaving aside the others – Carthage in its prime
measured twenty-four miles in circumference, and Rome fifty, not
counting its suburbs, which were almost endless, extending in one
direction as far as Ostia, in the other almost to Otricoli,[23] and cov-
ering vast expanses of land on all sides. But let us pass on, for this
chapter also refers to everything we will discuss below pertaining
to the prince's residence.

## 11. On the Residence of the Nobility

Among several reasons why cities in Italy are generally bigger than
those in France or other parts of Europe, it is of no small significance that in Italy the nobles live in the cities, whereas in France

---

23   Botero exaggerates the size of Rome. Ostia is at the mouth of the Tiber; Otricoli is a
     village near Narni in southern Umbria.

they reside in their country castles, which are usually buildings surrounded by moats full of water, with walls and towers strong enough to withstand a sudden assault. Even though Italian nobles may also live splendidly in country villas, as one can see in the territories of Florence, Venice or Genoa, which are full of buildings whose fine materials and excellent workmanship would do honour to a kingdom, let alone a city, nevertheless buildings of this sort are always grander and more numerous in France than in Italy. This is because an Italian divides his money and his attention between the city and the country, caring more for the former than the latter, while the Frenchman displays all his power in the countryside, and cares little or nothing for the city, where in any case an inn is enough for him. Now when nobles reside there, cities become more renowned and more populous, not only because the nobles' families live there with them, but even more because a baron spends his money much more freely when he is emulating his fellow nobles and vying with them in a city, where he constantly sees and is seen by people of quality, rather than in the country, where he lives among animals, converses with peasants, and goes about dressed in coarse cloth or linen. And so of necessity buildings increase and craftspeople multiply in a city.

For this reason, in order to glorify and expand his royal city of Cusco, the Inca of Peru did not merely desire that his caciques and barons would reside there, but issued an order for each one to build his palace there, which they did in competition with each other, so that the city grew greatly in a short time. Certain dukes of Lombardy have attempted the same thing in our own day. King Tigranes of Armenia,[24] when he built the great city of Tigranocerta, compelled a great many gentlemen and persons of rank and wealth to move there with all their goods, and moreover issued a proclamation that any possessions they did not convey there would be confiscated, if found anywhere else. This too is the

---

24   Reigned 94–55 BCE.

reason why Venice grew so rapidly at its beginning: because the people from the surrounding region who sought refuge in the little islands where the city is almost miraculously situated were rich and well born, and brought all their wealth with them, which they employed in navigation and trade, benefiting from the city's favoured position on the Adriatic Sea. In a short time they became the lords of the city and the nearby islands, and with their riches it was easy for them to adorn their fatherland with grand buildings and priceless treasures, and they have finally brought it to that degree of power and grandeur in which we see and admire it today.

## 12. On the Residence of the Prince

For the same reasons that we advanced just before, in the chapter on dominion, it is of immeasurable assistance in making a city great and magnificent if the prince resides there. The city grows as the prince's empire grows, because where he resides there too will be the parliaments, or senates as they are called, which are the highest courts of justice, and the secret councils of state. All important business converges there, every prince and person of importance, the ambassadors of republics and kings, and the agents of the subject cities; aspirants rush there to compete for state offices and honours; and the state's revenues are brought there and dispensed, as one can easily see from the examples of almost every city of significance and repute.

Egypt was a very ancient kingdom whose rulers held sway partly in Thebes and partly in Memphis, with the result that both cities rose to notable grandeur and beauty. Thebes, poetically called by Homer the hundred-gated city, measured seventeen miles around according to Diodorus Siculus;[25] it was embellished with wonderful

---

25  A compiler of histories, first century BCE.

buildings, public and private, and was crowded with people; and Memphis was only slightly smaller. In later centuries the Ptolemies fixed their seat at Alexandria, which therefore increased in the number of its buildings and population, in renown and extraordinary wealth, while the other two cities, because of the ruin of the kingdom of Egypt, conquered first by the Chaldeans and then by the Persians, were much reduced, and almost completely deserted. The sultans of Egypt subsequently abandoned Alexandria and withdrew to Cairo, which in a few centuries became so populous that for good reason it acquired the title of "great." The sultans, because they did not feel safe surrounded by innumerable multitudes of people who might rise up against them, divided up the city with many broad ditches full of water, so that it appeared to be many little towns clustered together, rather than a single city.[26] It is said that it had sixteen thousand great streets, or eighteen thousand according to Ariosto,[27] which are closed at night with gates of iron. It may measure eight miles in circumference, and within this area a countless multitude lives, because those people do not live as comfortably as we do, with room to spare, but for the most part on the ground, crammed and crowded together. The plague is hardly ever absent, but every seventh year it really makes itself felt, and if then it carries off less than three hundred thousand people it is considered a jest. At the time when the sultans reigned, the city was considered healthy if no more than a thousand people died in a day.[28] And that is enough to say about Cairo, which today is so famous throughout the world. But let us pass on.

In Assyria the kings made their residence at Nineveh, so that according to Diodorus the city measured four hundred and eighty

---

26  The 1588 and 1589 editions add: "today it is divided into three main parts, which are almost a mile apart, and are called Bulacco, Old Cairo and New Cairo."

27  *Orlando furioso*, XV, 63.

28  Botero is referring to the Mameluke sultans who ruled before the Ottoman conquest in 1517.

*stades* around,[29] which makes sixty miles, and was one hundred and fifty *stades* in length. It must also have had enormous suburbs, because Scripture states that three days were required to traverse it.[30] The residence of the Chaldean kings was in Babylon, which Herodotus tells us was four hundred and eighty *stades* in circumference; its walls were fifty cubits thick and two hundred or more high. According to Aristotle it was even bigger, for he writes that after Babylon fell it was said that the news did not reach one part of the city for three days;[31] it had a hundred gates, all of bronze, and a citadel or fortress twenty *stades* in circumference; its population was so numerous that it dared to offer battle against Cyrus, the very powerful king of Persia. Semiramis built the city, but it was Nebuchadnezzar who wondrously enlarged it.[32] It was ruined in the invasion of that country by the Scythians and other peoples, and was rebuilt by a certain Bugiafar,[33] the caliph of the Saracens, at a cost of eighteen million *scudi*. Paolo Giovio writes that even today it is bigger than Rome, if you consider the circuit of its ancient walls, but this area includes fields and forests for hunting, as well as orchards and spacious gardens.[34] The Medean kings resided at Ecbatana, and the Persian kings at Persepolis, about whose size we have no way of knowing beyond conjecture. In our own time the kings of Persia make their residence in Tauris,[35] and since their empire is not as great as it once was, neither is their capital city. Even so it extends about sixteen miles around, although some say it is more than that, and is quite long as well; it

---

29  A classical Greek measure of distance, equivalent to 175–200 metres.
30  Jonah III, 3: "Ninive erat civitas magna itinere trium dierum" (Nineveh was a great city of three days' journey).
31  *Politics*, III, 1 (1276).
32  Semiramis was a mythical queen of Babylon. Nebuchadnezzar reigned 605–562 BCE.
33  Abu Jafar abd-Allah al-Mansur, the second Abbasid Caliph (r. 754–75). He was the founder of Baghdad, which Botero here confuses with Babylon.
34  Paolo Giovio, *Dell'historie del suo tempo*, Book XXXIII.
35  Tabriz.

has many gardens and is without walls, as is normal for almost all the cities in Persia.

In Tartary and eastern Asia, because the rulers there are extremely powerful, the cities are bigger than anywhere else in the whole world. The Tartars today have two great empires: one is that of the Mughal Tartars, the other the Cathayans.[36] In our time the Mughals have expanded their domains to an unbelievable extent, because Muhammad their prince,[37] not content with his original boundaries, a few years ago conquered and occupied all the land between the Ganges and the Indus. The capital city of the Mughal Tartars is Samarkand, which the great Tamerlane incredibly enriched with spoils from the length and breadth of Asia where, like a fearful tempest or a raging flood, he destroyed the noblest and most ancient cities and carried off their wealth; to speak of just one city, from Damascus alone he took away eight thousand camel-loads of plunder and precious furnishings. Samarkand was so great and powerful that in some old reports we read that it fielded sixty thousand horsemen, but today it is not as great and splendid because the empire has diminished. After the great Tamerlane's death the empire was immediately divided into many parts by his sons, just as in our own time it has been divided once again between the sons of Muhammad, who recently subjugated Cambay.[38]

But since I have mentioned Cambay, there are two cities worthy of note in that kingdom: one is Cambay itself, and the other is Chitor.[39] Cambay is so great that it has given its name to the entire

---

36  Botero calls them the Mogori and the Cataini. "Cataini" refers to the region called Cathay by Marco Polo. Botero was evidently unaware that the Mongol (Yüen) dynasty that ruled China from 1279 to 1367 had been overthrow by the Ming, the dynasty that ruled China at the time he was writing. He treats "Cathay" (northern China) and what he calls "China" (the coastal region of South China) as separate countries.

37  Zahir ud-Din Muhammed, or Babur (1483–1530), founder of the Mughal empire.

38  The kingdom of Gujarat in western India, invaded in 1537 by Sultan Humayun (1508–56), son of Babur, and reconquered by Sultan Akbar (1542–1605) in 1572. It is not clear which of these conquests is referred to here.

39  Khambat, on the gulf of the same name, and Chittorgath in Rajasthan, both in western India.

province; some write that its population numbers one hundred and fifty thousand households, which would amount to almost eight hundred thousand inhabitants, reckoning the usual five persons for every household. Others put the figure much lower, but it is nevertheless a very famous city, the capital of a very rich kingdom and the residence of a very powerful king, who led an army of five hundred thousand foot soldiers and one hundred and fifty thousand cavalry, thirty thousand of them armed like our men-at-arms, in the campaign against Muhammad, the king of the Mughals. Chitor measures twelve miles around, and is so full of magnificent buildings, beautiful streets and pleasure-parks, that few other cities equal it, and those people call it "the shadow of heaven." In our day it was the capital city of Queen Crementina, who rebelled against the king of Cambay, and was violently over-thrown by him in 1536.[40]

The emperor of the Cathayan Tartars, commonly called the Great Khan of Cathay, is descended from the great Genghis Khan, who issuing forth from Scythian Asia almost three hundred years ago now, was the first to bring glory to the name of the Tartars by the grandeur of his exploits and his valour in battle. He sub-jugated China, made a large part of India his tributary, crushed Persia, and caused all of Asia to tremble. The successors of this great prince make their residence at Ciambalù,[41] a city as vast as it is magnificent, for it is said to measure twenty-eight miles around, not including the suburbs. Its trade is so extensive that every year, in addition to the other merchandise, close to a thousand cartloads of silk are brought in from China, from which one can gauge the scale of its commerce, the richness of its merchandise, the variety of the crafts practised there, and the number, splen-dour, refinement and elegance of its inhabitants.

---

40  Presumably Rani Karnavati, defeated by Sultan Bahadur of Gujarat.
41  I.e., Khan balik, "the khan's residence," founded by Kublai Khan, today Beijing. Botero failed to recognize that they were the same city (below he describes "Pan-chin" or Beijing as a different city), and (following Marco Polo) believed that the Mongol khans still ruled there.

Let us now proceed into China. There has never been a kingdom as extensive as China (I am speaking of kingdoms that are united and form so to speak a single whole), nor as populous, nor as rich and plentiful in every necessity, nor one that has continued in existence for as many centuries as this. Consequently, the cities in which its rulers have resided are the largest that have ever existed in the world, and they are three: Suntien, Anchin and Panchin.[42] Suntien, as far as I understand, is the oldest of them, and is the capital of a province called Quinsai, the name by which this city is commonly known. It is situated in nearly the easternmost region of the country, on a vast lake that is fed by four royal rivers flowing into it, the most famous of which is called the Polisango.[43] The lake is full of little islands, and is extraordinarily pleasant by reason of its beautiful situation, the coolness of its air, the views of its buildings and the loveliness of its gardens; its banks are carpeted with greenery and covered with trees, watered by clear streams and broad springs, and adorned with stately palaces; the mouth of the lake is four leagues across at its broadest point, but in some places it is no more than two leagues wide. The city is about twenty-eight miles from the mouths of the rivers, and is about a hundred miles around, with broad highways by both land and water; all those on land are paved with stone and are decorated with very fine benches where one can sit. Its most famous canals number perhaps fifteen, with such fine bridges that ships can pass beneath them in full sail; the main canal passes almost through the middle of the city and is more or less a mile wide, with perhaps eighty bridges, and there is nothing more beautiful or more convenient to behold. It would be a lengthy matter for me to set down everything that can be said about the grandeur of its

---

42    Evidently Songjiang, Nanjing, and Beijing. Botero apparently conflates Songjiang
      with nearby Quinsai or Hangzhou, described by Marco Polo, whose account he fol-
      lows in part here.
43    Today the river Lougou, near Beijing. Botero erroneously places it near Hangzhou.

squares, the magnificence of the palaces, the beauty of the streets, the inestimable multitude of inhabitants, the endless concourse of merchants, the uncountable numbers of ships, decorated with ebony and ivory, and also with gold and silver, the boundless riches that perpetually enter and leave the city, and finally all the pleasures that this city has to offer, for which it deserves the proud title of the "heavenly city." But both Panchin and Anchin are no smaller than this city.

But since we have referred to China, it may be proper here to recall the vast scale of some of its other cities, according to the reports we have received up to the present. Canton, which is the most famous but not the biggest of them, is admitted by the Portuguese, who have been carrying on an extensive trade there for several years now, to be bigger than Lisbon, which itself is the largest city in Europe, apart from Constantinople and Paris. Sauchieo is said to be three times as big as Seville, so if Seville encompasses six miles, Sauchieo will be seen to encompass eighteen. It is said that Ucchieo is bigger still. Chinchieo, though of only middling size, appeared to the Augustinian Fathers who saw it to be a city of seventy thousand households.[44] These things should not seem incredible to anyone because, besides Marco Polo's description, which asserts even greater things, today they are so clear from the reports that constantly reach us from the clerics, both regular and secular, and from all the Portuguese nation who traffic there, so that denying them would make one appear foolish rather than judicious. But in order to entertain and satisfy my readers it will not be difficult for me to examine the reasons why China is so populous, and so full of stupendous cities.

Let us suppose then, that either through the beneficence of heaven, or because of some occult influence of the stars that is

---

44    "Sauchieo" is probably Suzhou in the Yangtze delta region; "Ucchieo" is probably Hangzhou, actually the same city as "Suntien" above; "Chinchieo" is probably Zhangzhou in the province of Fujien.

beyond our knowledge, or for some other reason, whatever it may be, the region of the world which to us is the Orient possesses I know not what virtue in the production of certain things that is greater than that of other places, so that in that happy region many excellent commodities grow that are completely lacking in the other regions, such as cinnamon, nutmeg, cloves, pepper, camphor, sandalwood, incense, aloe and Indian nuts, and other such things. Furthermore, things that are common to both East and West all attain greater perfection there than here, as pearls, gold, diamonds, emeralds and bezoar stones attest, for pearls from the West when compared to those from the East seem almost as lead is to silver, and likewise the bezoar stone from India is far superior to what they bring us from Peru.[45] Now China is the most easterly part of the world that is known, for which reason it enjoys all the perfections attributed to the Orient, and firstly the air, which is more important for life than anything else, aided by the proximity of the sea, which surrounds and as it were embraces that country, penetrating a long way inland through a myriad bays and inlets, making it generally temperate. The country itself is mostly flat, and by its nature admirably suited to the production of every kind of delicacy, no less than all the things necessary to sustain life. The mountains and hills are perpetually clothed with all kinds of trees, some wild, some bearing fruit, and the plains with rice, barley, wheat and vegetables. The gardens, besides other kinds of the fruits that we know, provide the most delicious melons, delicate plums, perfect figs, lemons and oranges of different types, and of an excellent flavour. They also have a herb from which they obtain a delicious juice, which they consume instead of wine, and which preserves and keeps them safe from those ills caused among us by the excessive consumption of wine.[46] Flocks and herds, birds and

45   A concretion found in the stomachs of some ruminant animals, with supposed properties as an antidote.
46   Presumably tea.

game abound, and infinite quantities of fine wool and leather, cotton, linen and silk. There are mines producing gold, silver and excellent iron. Very fine pearls are found there. Sugar, honey, rhubarb, camphor, red lead, woad, musk, aloes and chinchona are plentiful; their porcelain is not made anywhere else.

Rivers and waterways of every kind run throughout the land, with inexpressible convenience for navigation and agriculture, and fish are as abundant in these waters as fruits are on land, because both the rivers and the sea yield an inexhaustible quantity. Such fertility of both soil and water is assisted by intensive cultivation, through which the maximum yields are obtained from both elements, and this is due to two reasons: first, the unbelievable number of the inhabitants, for it is estimated that China's population may exceed sixty million souls; secondly, the great diligence both of the people who till their farms and reap their produce, and of the magistrates who do not allow anyone to be idle or unemployed, with the result that there is not a foot of land that is not extremely well cultivated. There is no need to speak of handicrafts, for there is no country where they flourish in greater variety and excellence, for two reasons: the first has already been mentioned, which is that everyone is compelled to perform some kind of work, even the blind, the maimed and the crippled, as long as they are not completely incapacitated; and by a law issued by Vitei,[47] king of China, women are obliged to follow their father's trade, or if they are noble or well born, to ply the distaff or the needle. The other reason is that children are required to learn their father's trade, so that there is an infinite number of artisans, and both young boys and girls know how to work almost from the day they are born, so that the crafts attain the highest degree of perfection. They allow nothing to go to waste: they use the manure of buffaloes, cattle and other animals to feed the fish, they

---

47   Perhaps a corruption of the title "huangdi," meaning "august ruler" or emperor.

use the bones of dogs and other animals to make sculptures, as we carve ivory, and they use rags and old cloth to make paper.

And finally the products of the land and of human ingenuity are so plentiful and so varied that they have no need of things from other countries, and they send a very great quantity of their products to foreign lands. To speak of only one thing, the amount of silk that is taken out of China is beyond belief; every year three thousand quintals[48] are taken by the Portuguese Indies, fifteen ships are loaded with silk for the Philippines, an incalculable quantity is sent to Japan, and an equal quantity to Cathay, as can be understood from what we said earlier about the amount imported to Ciambalù.[49] They sell their manufactures and finished goods so cheaply, because they produce them in such infinite quantities, that the merchants from New Spain who come to buy these goods in the Philippine Islands, where the Chinese go to trade, are astounded. For this reason the Philippines trade produces more loss than profit for the Catholic King, since the high quality of the Chinese merchandise leads the people of Mexico, who used to supply themselves with various goods from Spain, to obtain them now from the Philippines. But His Majesty makes no account of these losses, because of his desire to win over those peoples, plunged in the awful darkness of idolatry, and draw them to the bosom of the Catholic Church.

From what we have said above it can be seen how China possesses the means, partly thanks to nature and partly thanks to human industry, to support an enormous population, and therefore we may believe that it is as well populated as we are told. Let me now add that this must be true, for two reasons: one is that the king of China is not permitted to make war in order to

48   A measure equivalent to 100 pounds.
49   Here again, following Marco Polo, Botero seems to treat "Cathay" or northern China, and southern China or "China" as separate countries.

conquer new lands, but only to defend his own, which means that they enjoy an almost permanent state of peace, and nothing is more fruitful than peace; the other reason is that the Chinese are not allowed to leave their country except with the permission of the magistrates. Since the number of people is constantly increasing, and none of them leave, it follows that the population must be beyond counting, and that in consequence, the cities are very big and the towns innumerable, or rather, that China is almost a single city.

In truth we Italians are too fond of ourselves and are too much the uncritical admirers of our own ways, when we prefer Italy and its cities over all the rest of the world. The shape of the Italian peninsula, long, narrow and bisected by the Apennines, and its scarcity of navigable rivers, do not allow it to contain any really big cities. I do not need to say that Italy's rivers are but rivulets in comparison to the Ganges, the Menan, the Mekong and the others, and that the Tyrrhenian and Adriatic Seas are mere ponds compared to the Ocean, so that in consequence our commerce is trifling when set against the markets of Canton, Malacca, Hormuz, Lisbon, Seville and the other cities situated on the Ocean. Add to this the enmity and conflict between ourselves and the Muslims that exclude us almost completely from trade with Africa, and largely from the Levant trade. Then the choicest parts of Italy, that is to say the Kingdom of Naples and the Duchy of Milan, are subject to the king of Spain, while the other Italian states are of middling size, as are their capital cities. But it is time now to return to where we started.

Such is the power and effect of a princely residence that on its own it is sufficient to establish and shape a city by itself alone. Francisco Alvares[50] writes that in Ethiopia there is no town bigger

---

50  A Portuguese cleric (1465–1536/41), sent in 1515 as the king of Portugal's envoy to Ethiopia, where he remained until 1526. His account of Ethiopia was published in 1540 and was translated into many languages.

than one thousand six hundred households, notwithstanding the vastness of the country, and that there are few towns of even this size. Because of this the king, whom the Ethiopians call the Great Negus, and whom we incorrectly call Prester John, has no fixed residence; he and his court alone represent a very big city, for wherever he goes he covers many miles of the country with an endless array of tents and pavilions. In Asia the cities worthy of note have all been the seats of rulers: Damascus, Antioch, Ankara, Trebizond, Bursa and Jerusalem.

But let us turn to our own Europe. The transfer of the imperial capital diminished Rome and made Constantinople great, and it has maintained its greatness and majesty as the residence of the Grand Turk. This city is placed in the most beautiful and most convenient site on earth, situated in Europe but no more than four hundred paces from Asia. It commands two seas, the Black Sea and the Sea of Marmara; the former has a circumference of two thousand seven hundred miles, and the latter extends for more than two hundred miles before it joins the Archipelago. The weather cannot be so rough and stormy that it halts maritime traffic and prevents the movement of goods from either sea to this most splendid city, and if it possessed a great, navigable river it would lack for nothing. Its walls extend for thirteen miles and enclose about seven hundred thousand people, although the plague carries off a great number every third year, and never really goes away. Why the plague should break out so violently there every third year, like a tertian fever (as it does in Cairo every seventh year), is a question that merits reflection, especially considering that Constantinople is situated in a very healthy location. But let us set this speculation aside for some other time, or leave it to a greater mind. In Constantinople there are seven hills, and on the side facing east, on the edge of the sea, stands the seraglio of the Grand Turk, whose walls are three miles around; there too is the arsenal with more than one hundred and thirty arches.[51] Finally for

---

51 The vaulted docks for galleys.

the beauty of its site, the convenience of its harbour, its access to
the sea, the multitude of its inhabitants, its enormous commerce,
and especially for its being the residence of the Grand Turk, Constantinople undoubtedly merits the first place among the cities of
Europe, because the court of that prince alone, between infantry
and cavalry, numbers no fewer than thirty thousand armed men.

In Africa, Algiers recently became the capital of a great state and
is therefore very well populated. Tlemcen in its heyday counted
sixteen thousand households, the city of Tunis nine thousand,
Morocco[52] one hundred thousand; Fez, which is now the seat of
the most powerful ruler in Africa, numbers sixty-five thousand
households.[53]

Among the kingdoms of Christendom (I refer to those that are
united and form a single whole), the largest, richest and most populous is France, for it has twenty-seven thousand places with parish
churches,[54] sustains fifteen million souls, and is so fertile through
the blessings of nature and so wealthy through the industriousness of its people, that it has no reason to envy any other country.
The residence of the kings of such a great realm has long been
Paris, with the result that it is the biggest city in Christendom; it is
twelve miles in circumference and numbers about four hundred
and fifty thousand inhabitants, whom it feeds with such plentiful
foodstuffs, and such a supply of all kinds of delicacies and good
things, that anyone who has not seen it cannot imagine it.

The kingdoms of England, Naples, Portugal and Bohemia, the
county of Flanders and the duchy of Milan, are states that are almost equal in size and power, so that the cities in which the rulers of those countries have established their residence are almost
equal too: London, Naples, Lisbon, Prague, Milan and Ghent,
each count more or less a hundred and sixty thousand souls. It is
true that the trade with Ethiopia, India and Brazil makes Lisbon

---

52  I.e., Marrakesh.
53  This sentence did not appear in the 1588 edition.
54  Here the editions of 1589 and 1590 add: "and I count Paris as one parish."

somewhat larger than the others, as the revolutions in the Low Countries have increased London, while over the last thirty years Naples has grown almost as much.

In Spain there is no city of comparable size, partly because up to the present the country was divided into small kingdoms, and because the lack of rivers and waterways makes it impossible to convey the provisions required to maintain an exceptional number of people to any one place. The cities however that are the most reputed and magnificent are those where the kings and princes used to reside: Barcelona, Saragossa, Valencia, Cordova, Toledo, Burgos, León, all of them renowned and quite populous, but none of them surpassing the cities of the second rank in Italy. Granada, which the Moors ruled for a long time and beautified with many fine buildings, surpasses these other cities. It is situated partly on a mountain, partly in the plain; the mountainous part consists of three hills, each one separated from the others. It is well supplied with all kinds of water, which is used to irrigate much of its very pleasant territory, and as a result it is so thickly populated and so well cultivated that there is none better. Seville has grown greatly since the discovery of the New World, because it is the destination for the fleets that each year bring such a quantity of treasure there that it is beyond estimation. The city measures six miles in circumference and has a population of eighty thousand or more. It is situated on the left bank of the river Betis,[55] or as we call it, the Guadalquivir, and is adorned with very beautiful churches and splendid palaces; the surrounding countryside is as fertile as it is pleasant. Valladolid is not a city but it can bear comparison with the finest cities in Spain because the Catholic King made his residence there for a long time, just as Madrid has now grown and is constantly growing because King Philip holds his court there, which is so effective in attracting great numbers of people that

---

55   The Latin name for the Guadalquivir.

it has transformed this place from a village into one of the most populated cities in Spain, even though its territory is not productive and the countryside is not pretty.

Cracow and Vilna are the most populous cities in Poland, because the former was the seat of the dukes of Poland, and the latter the seat of the grand dukes of Lithuania.[56] In the empire of Muscovy there are three very large cities, Vladimir, Novgorod the Great, and Moscow, since they were all the seats of grand dukes and the capitals of great domains. Today the most famous is Moscow, because the grand duke makes his residence there. The city is perhaps five miles long, but not so wide, with an enormous castle that serves as the court and the palace of that prince, and it is so populous that some place it among the four cities of the highest rank in Europe, which in their judgment are Constantinople, Paris and Lisbon, along with Moscow.

In ancient times the biggest city in Sicily was Syracuse which, as Cicero writes,[57] was divided into four districts, each of which could be considered a good-sized city in its own right. The reason for its greatness was that the kings, or tyrants as they might be, made their residence there. But after the infidel invasions cut off trade to North Africa, the royal seat was transferred to Palermo, which has continued to grow ever since, while Syracuse has declined. Palermo is equal to the cities of the second rank in Italy; it is adorned with rich churches and magnificent palaces, and the remains of various buildings erected by the Saracens. More noteworthy however are two modern things: one is the street that passes through the entire city, so straight, broad and long, and flanked with such beautiful buildings, that I do not know which city in Italy has one like it, and the other is the breakwater, constructed at inestimable expense, and thanks to which the city possesses a capacious

---

56  They merged in 1569 to form the Union of Lublin.
57  Cicero, *In Verrem*, IV, 53.

harbour – a construction worthy of the magnanimity of ancient Rome.[58]

But what reason have we to wander through other parts of the world in order to demonstrate how important the residence and dwelling place of a prince is for the greatness of a city? Would not Rome, the capital of the world, be more like a desert than a city if the Supreme Pontiff did not reside there, and magnify the city with his splendid court and the ambassadors, prelates and princes who flock there? And if he did not populate it with the infinite number of people from every nation, who have recourse to his authority or that of his ministers? And if he did not beautify it with magnificent buildings, aqueducts, fountains and streets? Or if he did not spend a great proportion of the Church's revenue on outstanding works, some for religious purposes, some for civil administration? And finally, if with all these things he did not attract and maintain such a number of merchants, shopkeepers, artisans and workers, and so many labourers and servants?

---

58    Botero had attended the Jesuit college at Palermo in 1559–60.

# BOOK III

## *I.*

The ancient founders of cities, considering that it is not easy to uphold law and civil order where there are large numbers of people, because multitudes engender confusion, therefore set limits to the number of citizens, beyond which they believed the form and the constitution of their cities could not be maintained: such were Lycurgus, Solon and Aristotle. But the Romans, believing that strength, without which a city cannot long maintain itself, derives chiefly from a numerous population, did all they could to increase and populate their city, as we demonstrated above, and at greater length in the book on *The Reason of State.*[1] If the world were ruled by reason, and if everyone were content with what justly belongs to them, it might be possible to follow the prescriptions of those ancient legislators, but experience, which teaches us that because human nature is corrupt, power prevails over reason and force of arms over law, also teaches us that the Romans' policy is to be preferred to that of the Greeks; and all the more when we see how the Athenians and the Spartans (not to mention the other Greek republics) were ruined by a minor setback involving the loss of seventeen hundred citizens, or a few more. The Romans however emerged victorious after losing most of their battles and campaigns, because when compared to their enemies, it is clear that far more Romans died in the wars against Pyrrhus and Carthage, or against Numantia, Viriathus, Sertorius and others.[2] But they triumphed as much because of their inexhaustible manpower, with which they recovered from their defeats

---

1  Book VIII, chapter 7.
2  The city of Numantia long resisted Roman attacks and was finally captured in 133 BCE. Viriathus was a leader of the resistance to Roman rule in the Iberian peninsula in the second century BCE. Sertorius (ca 122–72) was a Roman general who fought there during the civil wars.

and overwhelmed their foes, proud and courageous though these
were, as because of their valour.

In the previous books we explained the means by which a city
can raise itself to the highest grandeur that could be desired, so
nothing more remains to be said about what we set forth there.
Now, not because it is essential to the argument, but as an embel-
lishment to the work, we shall consider the following:

## 2. Why Cities Do Not Grow Proportionately

No one should believe that the means described above, or other
ones that might be discovered, could enable a city to grow indef-
initely. In fact a question worthy of consideration is why cities,
having attained a certain degree of power and greatness, do not
continue to grow, but stop at that point, or regress. Let us take
Rome as an example. At the beginning, when Romulus founded
the city, Dionysius of Halicarnassus[3] tells us that it could muster
three thousand, three hundred men able to bear arms. Romulus reigned for thirty-seven years, and during that time the figure
rose to forty-seven thousand fighting men. Under Servius Tullius,
about one hundred and fifty years after the death of Romulus,
eighty thousand men were listed as able to bear arms in Rome,
and little by little this number rose to a total of four hundred and
fifty thousand. I therefore ask how it was that the Roman people
increased from three thousand, three hundred fighting men to
four hundred and fifty thousand, but did not increase beyond that
number? Likewise, Milan and Venice had the same populations
four hundred years ago as they have today: so why did they not
multiply any further?

Some will reply that it is because of plagues, wars, famines and
similar causes, but this is not a sufficient explanation, because

---

3   *Antiquitates Romanae*, II, 16.

there have always been plagues, and wars were far more frequent and bloody in the past than in our own times. In those days armies would immediately come to hand-to-hand combat in an encounter on the field of battle, in which more men died in three or four hours than are slain nowadays in many years, because today warfare has moved from the open country to the walls of towns, and the spade is used far more than the sword. Then too the world has never been without alternations of famine and plenty, of plagues and healthy times, and I do not need to cite examples of this, for the history books are full of them. Now if cities that start out with a few inhabitants attain large populations, despite all these misfortunes, why do they not continue to grow at the same rate? Some will say that it is because God, Who ordains all things, disposes it in this way. No one doubts this, but since God in His infinite wisdom makes use of secondary causes to direct and govern nature, I ask by what means does eternal Providence cause the few to multiply, and place a limit on the many? To answer this question, let us say that it can also be asked about the human race as a whole: considering that in three thousand years it has multiplied from a single man and woman to such an extent that it has filled every province of the continents and the islands of the ocean, why has this increase not been greater over these three thousand years?

Let us settle this question insofar as it concerns cities, however, because that will also settle it for the world as a whole. Let us say, therefore, that cities grow in part because of the procreative power of human beings, and in part because of the cities' power to sustain them. It is beyond doubt that the procreative force has remained constant, at least for the last three thousand years, because human beings today are just as capable of reproducing as they were in the time of Moses or David, so that if there were no other obstacle, human beings would have propagated endlessly, and cities would have grown infinitely. So if the population fails to increase, we must conclude that this is the result of a lack of food and subsistence. Now a city's provisions are obtained either from its territory, or from abroad, so that if the city is to expand, its foodstuffs must be imported from far away. In order to draw provisions to it from distant places it must possess a force of attraction so powerful that it can overcome the roughness of the countryside, the height of the mountains, the depth of the valleys, the swiftness of the rivers, the perils of the sea, the attacks of pirates, the unpredictability of the winds, and the high costs and the bad condition of the roads; the jealousy of neighbours, the hatred of enemies and the rivalry of competitors; the length of time needed for transportation; shortages and the demands of the places from which the goods are brought; the innate enmity of other nations and the opposition of religious sects;[4] and other such things, which increase as the city's population and its needs increase. These obstacles finally become so many and so grave that they defeat all human effort and diligence, because how will it ever be worthwhile for merchants to ship grain to Rome from India or Cathay, for example? Or how could the Romans expect to get it from there? And even if both these parties could do this, who will give them assurances that the harvests will always be bountiful, that the different nations will remain at peace, that the mountain passes will be open and the roads will be safe? Or what means could be found to transport provisions to Rome for such a distance overland that the carriers could endure the fatigue and cover the cost? So if a single one of these obstacles is encountered, let alone several together, it is enough to scatter the population of a city in need, and prey to so many adverse circumstances. A shortage of food, a famine, a war, an interruption of commerce and business, a merchants' bankruptcy, or some other such thing will make the people seek another country, like swallows when winter comes.

The greatness of cities normally stops at the point at which it can be conveniently maintained, but greatness that results from

---

4   Here the editions up to 1596 added "to our religion."

remote causes or arduous efforts does not last for long, because everyone seeks their own ease and convenience. Add to this the fact that big cities are much more subject to famines than small ones, because they require larger quantities of provisions; they are also more vulnerable to the plague, because infection attacks them more easily and wreaks greater slaughter, and they are more prone to all the misfortunes we have enumerated, because they require more of everything.

So although people were just as capable of procreating at the height of Rome's power as they were at its beginning, nevertheless the population did not grow at the same rate, because the city's power to nourish its people was not strong enough to go any further. So with the passage of time, because the food supply did not increase, the inhabitants either failed to marry and set up households, or if they did, through hardship or penury their children lacked for everything and sought a better life far from their homeland. To solve this problem the Romans selected the poorest citizens and sent them out to colonies, where their living conditions would improve and they would consequently multiply, like transplanted trees. For the same reason the human race, once it reached a certain number, has not increased any further, and the world was as full of people three thousand years ago and more as it is today, because the fruits of the earth and the supply of food do not allow for a greater number of people.

Human beings began to propagate themselves in Mesopotamia, and as their numbers grew bit by bit they spread out in all directions; having filled up the mainland, they crossed over to the islands in the sea, and little by little from our countries they reached the lands we call the New World. Nothing is so bitterly fought over as land, subsistence and convenient places to live. The Suebi[5] considered it their glory to have laid waste their frontiers for many

---

5   An important confederation of Germanic peoples, from the second century BCE to the second century CE.

hundreds of miles. In the New World the inhabitants of Dominica and the neighbouring islands hunt other humans, as we do deer or hares, and feed on their flesh; many of the peoples of Brazil do the same, particularly those called the Aymuros; they tear apart boys and girls and eat them alive, and they also cut open the bellies of pregnant women, rip out the foetuses, and devour them in the presence of the fathers after roasting them over a fire, a thing that is horrible to hear, let alone to witness. Because of their poverty the people of Guinea every day sell their children for a very low price to the Moors, who carry them off to Barbary, and to the Portuguese, who transport them to their islands or sell them to the Castilians, to take to the New World. The people of Peru do the same, selling their children to anyone who wants them for next to nothing, because of their poverty, and their inability to rear and nurture them. The Tartars and Arabs live by plunder; the Nasamoni and Cafri, very barbarous peoples of Ethiopia, live off the spoils from the shipwrecks of others, as the Portuguese have discovered on more than one occasion. Moreover its is well known how many times the Gauls, the Teutons, the Goths, the Huns, the Avars, the Tartars and various other peoples, unable to live in their own countries because of their infinite numbers, went forth beyond their frontiers, occupied the lands of other peoples, and killed off the inhabitants. So it came about that in a few centuries almost all the countries of Europe and Asia were overrun by alien peoples who had left their homelands because of their excessive numbers, or because they wanted to live an easier and more plentiful life.

What is the chief cause of all the crowds of robbers and murderers but penury? What is the cause of quarrels and legal disputes, other than the narrowness of boundaries? What are we to conclude from the boundary markers, ditches, hedges and other defences placed around properties, the watchmen who guard vineyards and ripe fruit, the doors of houses, and the guard dogs that are kept there, except that the world is too small to satisfy

our needs or our greed? And what are we to say about all the
kinds of weapons there are, and how cruel they are? What shall
we say about the unending warfare on land and sea, the fortresses
at every pass, the walls of cities? Then add to these reasons bar-
ren soil, famines, baleful celestial influences, contagious diseases,
plagues, earthquakes, floods from rivers and from the sea, and
other such misfortunes, which by destroying now a city, now a
kingdom, now one people, now another, prevent the number of
human beings from increasing immoderately.

## 3. *On the Causes That Maintain a City's Greatness*

Now that we have brought our city to that degree of greatness
that is permitted by the nature of its site and the other factors that
we enumerated above, what remains is to preserve and maintain
it. Justice, peace and abundance all aid in this, because justice
secures each person's possessions, peace causes agriculture, commerce and crafts to flourish, and plentiful food makes subsistence
and life easier, for nothing makes the people happier than cheap
bread. Finally, all those things that are the causes of greatness are
also those that are best to assure its continuance, for the causes
that produce a thing and that preserve it are the same.

## A TREATISE. HOW MANY PEOPLE ROME MIGHT HAVE CONTAINED AT THE HEIGHT OF ITS GREATNESS[6]

As far as one can judge, Rome was one of the largest and most populous cities that have ever existed in the world, both because of the many policies employed to attain this end (for no other people took so much care to propagate itself), and because of the greatness of its empire, all of whose strength was gathered into the city. So it would not be amiss, since we are discussing the greatness of cities, for us to try to discover the total number attained by the people of Rome – which can be called the queen of cities – at its height.

Although this poses some difficulty, it is not insoluble, for if we can measure the size of the stars and the heavens from the shadow of the earth, we will much more easily estimate the size of Rome's population, using a far surer and clearer foundation, which is the census. Dionysius of Halicarnassus writes that during the consulate of Spurius Servilius and Aulus Virginius the number of male Roman citizens above the age of puberty had reached one hundred thousand, and that the total of women, children, shopkeepers (for it was unlawful for Roman citizens to pursue any occupation except farming and soldiering), and foreigners was three times greater, so that Rome could have had a population of four hundred thousand at that time.[7] Then we read that some centuries later Rome had grown to four hundred and fifty thousand citizens of the same age, from which, using the same ratio as above, we can conclude that the total number of people living in the city amounted to one million four hundred thousand. It is however likely that that this total was even higher, for the number of foreigners had greatly increased through the expansion of

---

6   Published as a separate pamphlet at Rome in 1588. Neither Peterson nor Hawkins includes it in his translation.

7   *Antiquitates Romanae* IX, 25. The census was taken in 485 BCE.

the empire, whereas at the time of the consuls named above the Romans were lords of no more than a very small part of Italy, so that the number of foreigners would not have been very large. But after Rome's armies had occupied all of Italy, traversed the Alps, crossed the seas and conquered the islands and countless provinces in Europe, Asia and Africa, it is probable that the number of foreigners who flocked to the city out of curiosity, or to do business, or for other reasons, would have been incalculable. Now a survey of the population of Athens was once made that enumerated twenty thousand citizens and ten thousand foreigners. It is unlikely that the number of foreigners was greater in Athens than in Rome, but let us suppose it was the same. If there were four hundred and fifty thousand citizens in Rome above the age of puberty, there could not have been fewer than one hundred and fifty thousand children below that age, and from this it would follow that the number of foreigners, using the same ratio as in Athens, would have amounted to almost three hundred thousand.

In addition, the enumerations of Rome's population did not include the slaves, who were there in enormous numbers, for we read that Marcus Crassus[8] possessed five hundred, all craftsmen, besides his personal servants; Milo[9] emancipated three hundred slaves in a single day; and the Blessed Paula,[10] so lauded by St Jerome, freed eight thousand slaves when she decided to withdraw into spiritual life;[11] that during Eunus's[12] war in Sicily with sixty thousand slaves he defeated four Roman praetors; that in Sicily too Athenion[13] with sixty thousand slaves defeated Servilius and Lucullus, who were also praetors; and the exploits of Spartacus,[14]

---

8   Marcus Licinius Crassus (ca 112–54 BCE), the richest man in Rome at that time.
9   Titus Annius Milo, Roman political figure, died in 48 BCE.
10   St Paula (374–404) withdrew to Bethlehem and founded a religious community there in 386.
11   St Jerome, *Epistolae* XXXIX and LXVI, in Migne, *Patrologia Latina*, vol. 22.
12   Leader of the first great slave revolt in Sicily, 135–2 BCE.
13   Leader of the second great slave revolt in Sicily, 101 BCE.
14   Leader of a slave revolt in southern Italy, 73–1 BCE.

who spread terror across Italy and cut many Roman armies to pieces, all attest to the same thing. After Sextus Pompeius[15] was defeated thirty thousand slaves were found to have joined his party, and they were put to death by Caesar Augustus. The survey of the Athenian population cited above listed four hundred thousand slaves in addition to the twenty thousand citizens and ten thousand foreigners. It is therefore probable that the Romans, who sword in hand had subjugated the entire world, were no less provided with slaves than the Athenians. From which we may conclude that the population of the city of Rome would have numbered close to two million people.

---

15   Son of Pompey the Great and an opponent of Augustus, who had him executed in 35 BCE.

# Bibliography of Works Cited

## Primary Sources

Barocchi, Paola, ed. *Scritti d'arte del Cinquecento*. 3 vols. Milan-Naples: Ricciardi, 1971–7.

Bodin, Jean. *Les six livres de la république*. 6 vols. Ed. Christiane Frémont, Marie-Dominique Couzinet, and Henri Rochais. Paris: Fayard, 1986.

Botero, Giovanni. *Discorso de vestigii, et argomenti della fede catholica: Ritrovati nell'India da' Portoghesi, e nel mondo nuovo da' Castigliani. Di Giovanni Botero benese*. Rome: Giovanni Martinelli, 1588.

Botero, Giovanni. *Ioannis Boteri benensis. De praedicatore verbi Dei, libri quinque . . .* Paris: G. Chaudiere, via Iacobaea, sub Temporis. & Hominis Silvestris, 1585.

Botero, Giovanni. *Della ragion di Stato di Giovanni Botero con tre libri Delle cause della grandezza delle città, due aggiunte e un discorso sulla popolazione di Roma*. Ed. Luigi Firpo. Turin: UTET, 1948.

Botero, Giovanni. *De regia sapientia libri tres. Quibus ratio reipub. benè, faeliciterque administrandae continetur . . .* Milan: Pacificum Pontium, 1583.

Botero, Giovanni. *Le relationi universali di Giovanni Botero benese, divise in quattro parti*. Venice: Giorgio Angelieri, 1600.

Brásio, Antonio, ed. *Monumenta missionaria Africana. Africa ocidental (1570–1599)*. 7 vols. Lisbon: Agencia Geral do Ultramar, 1958–2004.

Fontana, Domenico. *Della trasportatione dell'obelisco vaticano et delle fabriche di nostro signore papa Sisto V fatte dal cavallier Domenico Fontana. Libro primo . . .* Rome: D. Basa, 1590.

Guicciardini, Lodovico. *Descrittione di M. Lodovico Guicciardini Patritio Fiorentino, di tutti i Paesi Bassi, altrimenti detti Germania Inferiore*. Antwerp: Willem Silvius, 1567.

*Tre discorsi appartenenti alla grandezza delle città. L'uno di m. Lodovico Guicciardini.; L'altro di m. Claudio Tolomei.; Il terzo di m. Giovanni Botero.; Raccolti da m. Giovanni Martinelli*. Rome: Giovanni Martinelli, 1588.

## Translations and Adaptations

Draud, Georg. *Ioannis Boteri . . . Tractatus duo: Prior: De illustrium statu et politia, libris X. Posterior: De origine urbium, earum excellentia, & augendi ratione, libris III. . . . Ex italico primum in germanicum, atque exinde in latinum translati & multorum memorabilium accessione ac indice . . . aucti, auctore M. Georgio Draudi.* Oberursel: L. Zetzner, 1602.

Hawkins, Sir Thomas. *The Cause of the Greatnesse of Cities: Three Bookes. With Certaine Observations Concerning the Sea. Written in Italian, by Iohn Botero: And translated into English by Sir T.H.* London: Printed by E. P[urslowe] for Henry Sell, 1635.

Lunden, Ludolph Georg. *Johannis Boteri libri tres de origine urbium earum excellentia et augendi ratione quibus accesserunt Hippoliti a Collibus incrementa urbium sive de causis magnitudinis urbium liber unus.* Helmstadt: Johannis Heitmuller, 1665.

Peterson, Robert. *A Treatise, Concerning the Causes of the Magnificencie and Greatnes of Cities, Devided into three bookes by Sig: Giouanni Botero, in the Italian tongue; now done into English by Robert Peterson, of Lincolnes Inne Gent.* London: T. P[urfoot] for Richard Ockould and Henry Tomes, 1606. Reprint, Amsterdam and Norwood, NJ: Walter J. Johnson and Theatrum Orbis Terrarum, 1979.

Raleigh, Sir Walter. "The Causes That Concern the Magnificency of a City." In Thomas Birch, ed., *The Works of Sir Walter Raleigh, Kt. Political, Commercial and Philosophical; Together with His Letters and Poems . . .* 2 vols, vol. 2: 321–9. London: R. Dodsley, 1751.

Von Colli, Hippolyt. *Hippolyti a Collibus incrementa urbium: Sive de caussis magnitudinis urbium: Liber unus . . .* Hannover: Guilielmum Antonium, 1600.

Waley, Daniel P., trans. and ed. *Giovanni Botero. The Reason of State, and the Greatness of Cities, translated by Robert Peterson.* London: Routledge and Kegan Paul, 1956.

## Secondary Sources

Albónico, Aldo. "Le 'Relationi Universali' di Giovanni Botero." In Artemio Enzo Baldini, ed., *Botero e la "Ragion di Stato." Atti del convegno in memoria di Luigi Firpo (Torino, 8–10 marzo 1990).* Florence: Leo S. Olschki, 1992.

Assandria, Giuseppe. "Giovanni Botero. Note biografiche e bibliografiche." *Bollettino Storico-Bibliografico Subalpino*, vol. 28 (1926): 407–42; vol. 30 (1928): 29–63, 307–51.

Baldini, Artemio Enzo. "Jean Bodin e l'Indice dei libri proibiti." In Cristina Stango, ed., *Censura ecclesiastica e cultura politica in Italia tra Cinquecento e Seicento*, 79–100. Florence: Leo S. Olschki, 2001.

Baldini, Artemio Enzo. "Primi attacchi romani alla *République* di Bodin sul finire del 1588. I testi di Minuccio Minucci e Filippo Sega." *Il Pensiero Politico* 34, no. 1 (2001): 3–39.

Ballon, Hilary, and David Friedman. "Portraying the City in Early Modern Europe: Measurement, Representation and Planning." In David Woodward, ed., *The History of Cartography*, vol. 3, pt 1: 680–704. Chicago: University of Chicago Press, 2007.

Brotton, Jerry. *Trading Territories. Mapping the Early Modern World.* London: Reaktion Books, 1997.

Chabod, Federico. *Giovanni Botero* (1934). Reprinted in Federico Chabod, *Scritti sul Rinascimento*, 271–458. Turin: Einaudi, 1967.

Cosgrove, Denis. *Apollo's Eye. A Cartographic Genealogy of the Earth in the Western Imagination.* Baltimore: Johns Hopkins University Press, 2001.

De Bernardi, Mario. *Giovanni Botero economista (Intorno ai libri "Delle cause della grandezza delle città"). Con una postilla bibliografica.* Turin: Istituto Giuridico della Regia Università, 1931.

De Mattei, Rodolfo. *Il problema della "Ragion di Stato" nell'età della controriforma.* Milan and Naples: Ricciardi, 1977.

Descendre, Romain. *L'état du monde. Giovanni Botero entre raison d' État et géopolitique.* Geneva: Droz, 2009.

Descendre, Romain. "Raison d'État, puissance et économie. Le mercantilisme de Giovanni Botero." *Revue de Métaphysique et de Morale* 39, no. 3 (July-Sept. 2003): 311–21. http://dx.doi.org/10.3917/rmm.033.0311.

De Vries, Jan. *European Urbanization, 1500–1800.* Cambridge, MA: Harvard University Press, 1984.

Elliott, James. *The City in Maps: Urban Mapping to 1900.* London: The British Library, 1987.

Fara, Amelio. *Il sistema e la città. Architettura fortificata dell'Europa moderna dai trattati alle realizzazioni 1464–1794.* Genoa: SAGEP, 1989.

Fiorani, Francesca. "Post-Tridentine 'Geographia Sacra': The Galleria delle Carte Geografiche in the Vatican Palace." *Imago Mundi* 48, no. 1 (1996): 124–48. http://dx.doi.org/10.1080/03085699608592836.

Firpo, Luigi. "Ancora sulla condanna di Bodin." *Il Pensiero Politico* 14, no. 1 (1981): 173–86.

Firpo, Luigi. "Botero, Giovanni." In *Dizionario biografico degli Italiani,* 72 vols in process, vol. 13 (1971): 352–62. Rome: Istituto della Enciclopedia Italiana, 1960–.

Firpo, Luigi. "La fortuna di un piccolo capolavoro: Il *Delle cause della grandezza della* [sic] *città.*" *Studi Piemontesi* 6, no. 1 (Mar. 1977): 98–103.

Firpo, Luigi. "Giovanni Botero, l'unico gesuita 'da bene.' " In Luigi Firpo, *Gente di Piemonte*, 71–92. Milan: Mursia, 1983.

Firpo, Luigi. "Postfazione" to reprint of *Della ragion di Stato e Delle cause della grandezza delle città, Venezia 1598*. Bologna: Arnaldo Forni, 1990.

Firpo, Luigi. *Gli scritti giovanili di Giovanni Botero. Bibliografia ragionata*. Florence: Sansoni, 1960.

Firpo, Luigi. "Al servizio di Federico Borromeo." *Studi Piemontesi* 4, no. 1 (Mar. 1975): 34–47.

Gambi, Lucio. "Egnazio Danti e la Galleria delle Carte Geografiche." In Lucio Gambi, ed., *La Galleria delle Carte Geografiche in Vaticano*, 3 vols, vol. 1: 83–96. Modena: F.C. Panini, 1994.

Guidoni, Enrico, and Angela Marino. *Storia dell'urbanistica. Il Cinquecento*. Bari: Laterza, 1982.

Headley, John M. "Geography and Empire in the Late Renaissance: Botero's Assignment, Western Universalism, and the Civilizing Process." *Renaissance Quarterly* 53, no. 4 (Winter 2000): 1119–55. http://dx.doi.org/10.2307/2901458.

Kagan, Richard. *Urban Images of the Hispanic World, 1493–1793*. New Haven: Yale University Press, 2000.

Magnaghi, Alberto. *Le "Relazioni universali" di Giovanni Botero e le origini della statistica e dell'antropogeografia*. Turin: Clausen, 1906.

Meadows, Paul. "Giovanni Botero and the Process of Urbanization." *Midwest Sociologist* 20, no. 2 (May 1958): 90–5.

Meadows, Paul. "Giovanni Botero e il processo di urbanesimo." *Rivista internazionale di scienze sociali* series 3, vol. 29 (July-Aug. 1958): 328–36.

Meinecke, Friedrich. *Machiavellism. The Doctrine of Raison d'État and Its Place in Modern History*. Trans. Douglas Scott. London: Routledge and Kegan Paul, 1957. German original, *Die Idee der Staatsräson in der neueren Geschichte*. Munich and Berlin: Oldenbourg, 1924.

Merola, Alberto. "Altemps, Marco Sittico." In *Dizionario biografico degli Italiani*, 72 vols in process, vol. 2 (1960): 551–7. Rome: Istituto dell'Enciclopedia Italiana, 1960–.

Milanesi, Maria. "Le ragioni del ciclo delle Carte Geografiche." In Lucio Gambi, ed., *La Galleria delle Carte Geografiche in Vaticano*, 3 vols, vol. 1: 97–123. Modena: F.C. Panini, 1994.

Nuti, Lucia. "The Perspective Plan in the Sixteenth Century: The Invention of a Representational Language." *Art Bulletin* 76, no. 1 (Mar. 1994): 105–28. http://dx.doi.org/10.2307/3046005.

Schulz, Juergen. "Maps as Metaphors: Mural Map Cycles of the Italian Renaissance." In David Woodward, ed., *Art and Cartography. Six Essays*, 97–122. Chicago: University of Chicago Press, 1987.

Simoncini, Giorgio. *Roma. Le trasformazioni urbane nel Cinquecento. I. Topografia e urbanistica da Giulio II a Clemente VIII.* Florence: Leo S. Olschki, 2008.

Sjoberg, Gideon. *The Preindustrial City, Past and Present.* New York: The Free Press, 1960.

Spence, Jonathan. *The Memory Palace of Matteo Ricci.* New York: Penguin Books, 1985.

# Index